Speaking Out for America's Children

MILTON J. E. SENN

NEW HAVEN AND LONDON
YALE UNIVERSITY PRESS
1977

Copyright © 1977 by Yale University.
All rights reserved. This book may not be
reproduced, in whole or in part, in any form
(except by reviewers for the public press),
without written permission from the publishers.
Library of Congress catalog card number: 76-49756
International standard book numbers: 0-300-02107-0 (cloth)
                                    0-300-02113-5 (paper)

Designed by Sally Sullivan
and set in Times Roman type.
Printed in the United States of America by
Vail-Ballou Press, Inc., Binghamton, N.Y.

Published in Great Britain, Europe, Africa, and
Asia (except Japan) by Yale University Press,
Ltd., London. Distributed in Latin America by
Kaiman & Polon, Inc., New York City; in
Australia and New Zealand by Book & Film
Services, Artarmon, N.S.W., Australia; and in
Japan by Harper & Row, Publishers, Tokyo
Office.

To Katarina and Kristian Midelfort, who symbolize the aspirations, hopes, and needs of all children, and to Judith Schoellkopf, whose life in various ways has helped the cause of children, this book is dedicated with love and pride.

Contents

Acknowledgments   xi

Introduction   xiii

1   The Plight of American Children and Their Families   1

Lisbeth Bamberger Schorr   James L. Hymes, Jr.
Marian Wright Edelman   Benjamin Spock
Sheldon White   Urie Bronfenbrenner
Elizabeth Wickenden   Lee Salk   William Kessen
Lola Nash   Stephen Hess   Leon Eisenberg
Sibylle Escalona   Tom Levin   William M. Schmidt
Edward Zigler   William Smith   Kenneth Keniston
Walter Mondale   Sally Provence

2   Woe to the Parents Who Turn to the Experts   41

Milton J. E. Senn   Charles P. Gershenson
Myrtle McGraw   William Kessen
J. McVicker Hunt   Lois Barclay Murphy
Joseph Reid   Benjamin Spock   Judith Schoellkopf
Lois Meek Stolz   Orville G. Brim, Jr.
Jerome Kagan   David Elkind   Lee Salk
Boyd McCandless   Sheldon White

3 After Millions Spent on Research, What Do
   We Know about Children? 71

   Jerome Kagan   Elizabeth Wickenden
   Sheldon White   David Elkind
   Charles P. Gershenson   William Kessen
   Tom Levin   James L. Hymes, Jr.
   Myrtle McGraw   Joseph Reid   Philip Sapir
   Leona Baumgartner   David Shakow
   Marian Wright Edelman   Herbert Zimiles
   Alfred Baldwin   Edward Zigler

4 Can Scientific Knowledge Help Frame Our
   Social Policies for Children? 99

   Marian Wright Edelman   David Elkind
   Charles P. Gershenson   Orville G. Brim, Jr.
   Jule Sugarman   William Kessen   Sheldon White
   Judith Miller   Julius Richmond   Edward Zigler
   Robert Aldrich   Kenneth Keniston
   Walter Mondale   Herbert Zimiles   Albert J. Solnit

5 Have Social Scientists Changed Our Attitudes
   and Behavior toward Children? 121

   Joan Costello   J. McVicker Hunt
   Orville G. Brim, Jr.   Nicholas Hobbs
   James P. Comer

6 Should Research on Children Be Geared to
   Social Relevance? 131

   Sibylle Escalona   Jerome Kagan   Lester Sontag
   Harold Stevenson   William Kessen   Sheldon White
   Walter Mondale   Leon Eisenberg

CONTENTS

7 What Are the Priorities in the Battle to
Improve the Lives of Children? 141

Justine Wise Polier   Nicholas Hobbs   Albert Quie
Margaret Mead   Sheldon White   Robert Aldrich
Urie Bronfenbrenner   Elizabeth Wickenden
Kenneth Keniston   James P. Comer
Marian Wright Edelman   Lois Meek Stolz
Martha Phillips   Peter Sauer
Marian Radke-Yarrow   Edward Zigler
Julius Richmond   Benjamin Spock   Trude Lash
Abraham Bergman   Gilbert Steiner   Joan Costello
Sally Provence

8 What Tactics Can Help to Change America's
Policies toward Its Children? 171

Orville G. Brim, Jr.   Justine Wise Polier
Marian Wright Edelman   Carolyn Harmon
Joseph Reid   William Smith   Abraham Bergman
Leona Baumgartner   Donald Cohen
Edward Zigler   Nicholas Hobbs   Gilbert Steiner
Robert Aldrich   Walter Mondale

Afterword 199

Chronology of the Child Development Movement,
1902–1975 203

Selected Bibliography 209

Index of Names 213

Acknowledgments

A person who collects oral history material and fashions it into a book is viewed variously by critics as a compiler of biographies, an arranger of information, an annotator, and, if the critic is friendly toward that kind of enterprise, perhaps as an author.

This says something about the nature of the undertaking: that it entails more than the researching and writing of a manuscript by a single person with the help of a few others. The whole project involves many different people, from the beginning of the first interview to the time of "putting it to bed."

Hence it is impossible to acknowledge each person who gave assistance to me in the preparation of this book. But a few must be named because of their significant contributions.

It should be self-evident that the individuals who freely and unselfishly gave me time and substance in the recorded interviews of their recollections and then permitted me to quote them here comprise a special group. Their words are the corpus of the history. They represent the best in their professional fields; that they really care about children is manifest on every page of this book.

Elsa Wardell, a researcher-writer of uncommon ability and intuition about human behavior, helped greatly in arranging the contents of the book and in discerning the quotations which most aptly substantiate the plight of American children.

Dr. Peter D. Olch, deputy chief of the History of Medicine Division of the National Library of Medicine, served as curator of the oral history tapes and transcriptions and provided ongoing assistance and advice about their preparation and use.

Financial assistance was provided originally by the National Institutes of Health (Contract NIH-73-C-199). Later, a generous grant came from the Carnegie Corporation of New York, whose Barbara Finberg lent personal encouragement all along the way.

Dr. Judith Schoellkopf as always was a sustaining influence as benefactor and friend.

The oral history could not have culminated in this book without the stimulation, encouragement, and creative sense of Jane Isay of the Yale University Press. Her associate Lynn Walterick helped guide the manuscript through various editorial checks; she did this with a spirit of joy as well as with competence. Each member of the Press who was involved aimed to make the book a worthy testament of his or her, as well as my, concern for children and a step in effecting significant changes in their behalf.

To all these persons, as well as to those unnamed, I am deeply grateful.

Introduction

This book is about America's children. Americans who are not poor, black or brown, hungry, lonely, inadequately housed, without pleasant or constructive things to do, physically handicapped or sick and lacking good medical care do not know much about the lives of millions of those others. Only glimpses of their problems are caught through newspaper stories, TV documentaries, reports of philanthropic foundations and governmental and social agencies, or possibly through occasional spates of volunteer work. But even Americans who consider themselves more fortunate know from firsthand experience with their own children or from observations of their friends' children that the inadequacies of contemporary society adversely affect the lives of most American children in one way or another, regardless of their economic or social status.

We who work in what are now called "the human services" as doctors, psychiatrists, social workers, psychologists, educators, sociologists, political scientists, lawyers, and related professions are often involved in helping troubled children whom society has failed in some way, and some of us have been bold enough to believe that we might prevent their difficulties by using the medical model which has shown that if the cause of a disease is known, there is a reasonable chance of preventing it. But all of us have had to come up against the reality that social pathology is not like physical disease; attitudes, motives, and life styles are much less amenable to change by persuasion and other human influences than bacteria and viruses are to physical and chemical agents.

Nevertheless, since the great progressive movement began near the turn of the century, activists have been bucking the odds with concerted efforts to improve the lives of children. The hopes of those reformers lay in exposing the facts. Disillusioned with moral exhortation and aware that the old shibboleths about the "unworthy poor" defied reality, the progressives were convinced that if the facts were made known, improvements would follow. Robert Bremner has called them the "factual generation"—"Facts, facts piled up to the point of dry certitude, was what the American then needed and wanted." [1] Large numbers of the facts bore on the miserable condition of so many of the nation's children; they were printed and circulated widely in magazine articles, in bulletins of the National Child Labor Committee, and in such heart-rending books as Ernest Poole's *The Street: Its Child Workers* (1903) and John Sprague's *The Bitter Cry of Children* (1906).

But Americans were encouraged to believe that the future held great promise of improved conditions for children. One optimistic voice was that of Swedish feminist and social critic Ellen Key, who wrote in 1909 *The Century of the Child,* a proscriptive for the twentieth century and its children.

If there was any cement that held the progressive movement together, it was the child. He was the nation's greatest resource; as the best hope for a finer America, he above all else had to be nurtured and protected. In 1909 the first White House Conference on Children was held; it led to the creation of the Children's Bureau in 1912, which became the leading advocate for children in this country until the recent scattering of its components among other government agencies. Congress passed in 1916 its first legislation banning certain types of child labor, after years of effort and disappointment on the part of a huge coalition of citizens led by the indomitable National Child Labor Committee, which had been formed in 1904. During this period strides were made in health and nutrition; playgrounds and

---

1. *From the Depths: The Discovery of Poverty in the United States* (New York: New York University Press, 1956), p. 140.

parks were established; John Dewey's progressive education movement got under way and compulsory school laws were passed. Led by such estimable proponents as Jane Addams of Hull House and Lillian Wald of the Henry Street Settlement, social service was becoming an established and honored profession, and child psychiatry was taking hold. New principles for handling juvenile delinquents were introduced and provisions for widows' pensions were made in some states.

How much of this child welfare movement was influenced by new theories which had been developing about the nature of childhood is debatable. But the assumptions about the natural stages of children's growth which had been formulated by G. Stanley Hall (William Kessen has called Hall "without qualification the founder of child psychology in the United States"[2]) were certainly used to bolster arguments against child labor and for the provision of play areas for poor children. And Hall's biographer has pointed out that the Child Study Movement which Hall led in the 1880s and 90s had "created the matrix in which progressive education developed."[3]

After World War I, efforts to better the conditions for children were accelerated at least in part because of dismay over the wretched physical and educational condition of so many Army recruits—a state of affairs that the 1919 White House Conference on Children made every effort to publicize. Well-baby clinics were established, child guidance clinics proliferated, school health programs were instituted, mothers' pension programs were more widely adopted. In 1921 the Shepard-Towner Act, which provided grants to states to develop health services for mothers and children, was passed by Congress.

While the progressives had put their faith in amassing the facts, the postwar activists looked to science. With the advent of major accomplishments in medicine, biology, chemistry, and nutrition, it seemed logical to conclude that scientists could

2. *The Child* (John Wiley, 1965), pp. 147–48.
3. Dorothy Ross, *G. Stanley Hall: The Psychologist as Prophet* (Chicago: The University of Chicago Press, 1972), p. xiii.

make similar strides in improving the lives of children. Institutes—mostly connected with universities—for the study of children in all their developmental aspects were established in various parts of the country under the inspiration of Lawrence K. Frank, an economist, and with the initial funds of the Laura Spelman Rockefeller Memorial where Frank was then an executive. In a brief summation of his career (written in the third person) Frank said: "In 1923, he foresaw the need for systematic and intensive study of child growth and development and envisioned a nationwide plan for such research and for parent education. . . . His knowledge of the research needs in the field of human development, particularly of the development of the young child, was accompanied by a vision of programs in home and school, and agencies of child care, in which the needs of the whole child would be central. He recognized that not only was a sound program of child rearing and child care dependent upon research in these fields . . . but that it was necessary to establish a climate of opinion through various forms of adult education within which these findings could be translated into practice." With the establishment of the institutes, the Child Development Movement, which still carries on, was launched.

In a sense, the purpose of this book is to assess the success of many of the efforts that have been made in this country on behalf of children since the start of the Child Development Movement. I was a participant in its beginnings, and so this assessment is in some ways a personal one.

As a physician trained in pediatrics, I witnessed, beginning in the 1920s, the working of "miracle drugs" in saving lives of children sick unto death with infectious diseases; the prevention of the so-called common contagious diseases by prophylactic measures and improvement in public health; the abolition for many infants of the dreaded "summer complaint" (diarrhea) by improvements in sanitation and public health; and the prevention and amelioration of many other physical ills of infants and children by the use of biological and chemical therapics.

By the 1930s this great success in medicine, made possible for the most part by research in the physical sciences, fostered my belief and hope that research in the social sciences, which admittedly were still in their ascendency, would have similar beneficial influence on the psychological and social problems which increasingly seemed the concomitants of physical ill health.

By then it was apparent that physicians, especially pediatricians, had to be concerned about new problems which soon came to be labelled psychosomatic. Already then, probably because these were the days of the Great Depression, there were some who realized that the major components in the genesis of those conditions were the horrible social conditions under which many children and families lived, and the ways in which children were reared, cared for, and educated.

Among physicians, psychiatrists, especially those treating children, were the most aware of these relationships. Along with colleagues in social work, they emphasized the role society played in creating social pathology which in turn causes physical and mental breakdown. As clinicians they had to deal with the afflicted directly, hoping to cure, desirous always of preventing. Their natural allies should have been the social scientists. And at times clinical psychologists *were* colleagues, helping to assess behavior, measure aptitudes, and analyze personality development. But for the most part, psychologists, sociologists, and political scientists were busily engaged in building theories, devising tests, designing experiments, and conducting research, all of which may have been aimed at helping children (some day, some time) but mostly satisfied the aesthetic needs, the academic demands, the approval of peers, and a guarantee of an income for the living expenses of the research workers.

From 1936 to 1938, in a desire to broaden my understanding of human behavior and to take a step toward bridging the gap between medical and social science, I studied psychiatry and psychoanalysis. I had some chance to study with social scientists, particularly clinical psychologists and sociologists. Following such training, I returned to the department of pediatrics at Cornell-New York Hospital. There I also became associated with the department of psychiatry, setting up an institute of child development which brought together medical, biological, and social scientists with the aim of teaching physicians-in-training about human behavior, human development, and interpersonal relationships. In 1948 I was appointed by the Yale Corporation to establish the Child Study Center. The mandate of the Yale Corporation was clear. Study of the child was to be carried on by a variety of persons representing the social and medical sciences. The interdepartmental, interdisciplinary aspects were to be emphasized.

By the 1960s, I (like many other Americans, particularly those in the academic world) was aware of the civil rights movement, and aware too of the inequities, not only in civil and voting rights, but in the way children had opportunities to be reared, educated, and cared for. I learned at first hand from children in Mississippi and South Carolina that many were in trouble, primarily because they were poor, made worse when they were black. Even in New Haven there was plenty of evidence to show that too many children were not learning, that an unbelievable number were hungry and even malnourished, that the infant and maternal mortality rates of our country were out of line with the medical services that we proudly proclaimed the best in the world.

The decade of the sixties was, of course, the time of President Johnson's "war on poverty." The federal government called on the universities and colleges—especially those which had departments of child education, development, psychology, and psychiatry—for professional recruits to help plan new programs for "disadvantaged" children. As a consequence, new organizations, and a few older ones, became prominent influences in the lives of many poor families. Head Start, Home Start, day care, open class education and others became household words.

The Yale Child Study Center supplied consultants in child

development and education, in cognitive development and health. And in this process the staff appraised its roles, analyzed its functions, reexamined its aims, and measured its failures and successes in helping children. Consequently, changes were made in the kinds of children admitted to our nursery school: emphasis was focused now on children in foster care, most of whom happened to be black. In order to get a firsthand knowledge of conditions in the ghettos of New Haven, having been protected from such experiences in the cloistered world of academia, I became a physician in a day-care center, where I was responsible for the health supervision and physical examination of about forty children. This led to contacts with parents through classes in child care and nutrition and through home visits, all of which made me acutely aware, as I had not been previously, of the deplorable life conditions of so many poor children.

As I approached my retirement I felt a keen disappointment in our accomplishments viewed in the light of all the continuing unmet needs of children. Realizing that there was little more I could do professionally, I considered that I might be able to make a contribution in another way. I felt that after some fifty years the child development movement needed to take a look at itself. A lot of time, effort and money had been expended—to what result? It was important to get a fix on the condition of children *now,* on the results of parent education on which Lawrence Frank had pinned so many hopes, on what we have learned about children after conducting so much research on them, on the relevance of our knowledge to improving the lives of children. Above all, it seemed to me to be important to examine past failures and successes as a key to better results today and tomorrow.

And so, during the period between the late 1960s and early 1975, I collected a series of taped interviews with some ninety leaders in the children's field—research and clinical psychologists, pediatricians, social scientists, lawyers, lawmakers—and, toward the end, with a number of mothers in day-care centers.

The persons chosen were prominent in their professions, representatives of the most active and the best in their groups. Others equally qualified had to be omitted because of lack of money and time to enlarge the sample.

Each interviewee was invited to participate; I outlined to each my aim of collecting their opinions and placing their unedited comments in a national archive (The National Library of Medicine) for scholars to use in assessing segments of American social history. The core topics were named, but it was understood that the interviews would be "free floating" as other material, relevant to the discussion and of interest to the interviewee, was spontaneously produced.

The conversations usually began with the early life experiences of those interviewed, especially as those experiences related to careers. An analysis of those comments, along with a discussion of this procedure as historical method, has been published previously.[4]

The topics of concern which became the basis for this book were, in general: (1) the condition of children in need today in our country; (2) how people who work with and for children view their influence as researchers, writers, clinicians, lawmakers; and (3) what these experts propose now as remedies. The chapter headings compose the core areas discussed; the contents of each chapter consist of quotations from the interviews. Each speaker is introduced briefly at his initial appearance.

The people speak, as it were, rather than the author, whose objective was to select appropriate comments, and arrange them in a manner that would kindle the reader's interest and understanding and possibly inspire him to personally press for changes in our society which would improve the conditions of life of children.

Readers will find these appraisals candid, doubting, rueful.

4. Milton J. E. Senn, *Insights on the Child Development Movement*, Society for Research in Child Development Monograph Serial 161, vol. 40, nos. 3–4, 1975.

Yet the men and women whose best efforts are directed on behalf of this country's children are still hopeful of contributing to a progress which will someday eventuate in the era that Ellen Key forecast prematurely in 1909. We may yet see a century of the child.

1 The Plight of American Children and Their Families

Agony, which is not denied to any man, is given in strange ways to children.

　　Flannery O'Connor, The Artificial Nigger

LISBETH BAMBERGER SCHORR   *Lisbeth Schorr was trained in economics and has worked in the field of medical-care organization and the delivery of health-care services. She was on the staff of the Office of Economic Opportunity shortly after its inception and helped start the Neighborhood Health Center Program. At the time of the interview she was working with the Children's Defense Fund in Washington, and her major interest was in studying ways the fund might improve health services for children. She is knowledgeable about public policy design and interested in its implementation, particularly with respect to meeting the needs of the family, home, and child-rearing. She is still a consultant to the Children's Defense Fund of the Washington Research Project.*

I really find it very hard to understand the paradox that people *individually* do want something for their own children—they are concerned that their children should have it better than they did—and yet that it is so difficult to get some of the obvious needs of children met through social action. My husband did a documentary on CBS on social programs for children, and the working title they had for it was "Why do we hate our children?" because that's how it really comes out in the way we treat children in a lot of contexts. And he found in talking about it that people were terribly shocked: "We *don't* hate our children. We don't, we don't. Everybody loves children more than anything." And yet, we have absolutely outrageous things happening to children at public hands. It isn't only a few aberrant families that abuse children: we abuse children in jails; we abuse children in detention homes; we abuse children in institutions for the mentally retarded, and in schoolrooms. Our social arrangements for income distribution and employment, for education, housing, health and social services, reflect child abuse and neglect—as a matter of public policy.

THE PLIGHT OF AMERICAN CHILDREN

JAMES L. HYMES, JR. *James Hymes has had a "concern with the quality of living in the world" from the time he was an undergraduate student of political theory, philosophy, and international law and relations. He has long worked in the field of early-childhood education, first, as director of the Kaiser Child Service Centers in Portland, Oregon, during World War II, and later as professor of education and chairman of the Department of Childhood Education at the University of Maryland. He was also a member of the group that planned and established Head Start. For the past several years he has been a consultant in the field of early-childhood education and a freelance writer.*

Overwhelmingly, I think, youngsters grow up and have grown up through all these years under punitive conditions within the family, under competitive and dominating conditions within the school, under conditions of idleness in the community.

When I read the papers in Atlanta, which seem to be unusually full of the tales of people being held at gunpoint, hostages, kidnappers, violence, I don't think it's a mystery in every instance where this comes from. The experiences of early childhood are of very great significance in the ultimate establishment of healthy adult behavior. One of my basic articles of faith is that the quality of living for young kids is not a luxury or not something to be taken lightly because we are paying a terrible price for not succeeding in making it good for children.

We are living in an era in which we are so stingy publicly with children, so harsh publicly to children, so blind to children's needs. I think if one has to find some words to sum up our relationship to kids—we've "held out" on children. Let me just, for example, express my present irritation. This year we celebrate the ninety-ninth birthday of public kindergartens in the United States, next year the hundreth birthday. I almost never see a good kindergarten after one hundred years because I never see a kindergarten where the teacher isn't just swamped with kids—just swamped with kids—and where the teacher wouldn't say, "Well, if I could just cut the group" (and they often say, "in half"), because they have thirty-seven, thirty-eight. This is, what's the word, chintziness. We don't spend, we won't spend on kids. And today people are loving to say, "Well, money won't solve everything," which admittedly it won't but, boy, there are some things that money could help with greatly.

One of the terms that I am so deeply troubled by now in education—pardon such a nasty use of words—but people talk of a "glut of teachers." I think the word "glut" is one of life's ugly words. There's a desperate shortage of excellent teachers; there is a desperate shortage of any kind of teachers in the classroom and then a desperate shortage of all the supportive people who should be helping teachers do a job with kids. This goes back a little bit to the Head Start guidelines where there was a concept not only of people who would function with children in a classroom, but of public health nurses, of social workers, of psychological help, of pediatricians and a whole range of other people to support the child's life in the classroom. But we don't do it and therefore I think we pay a price as kids grow up.

MARIAN WRIGHT EDELMAN *As a black college student who had participated in the civil rights movement in the South in the 1960s, Marian Edelman resolved to sharpen her skills and to acquire new techniques in the legal profession to use in the struggle for equal rights for children, which she knew would be her lifelong pursuit. She has been innovative in planning and implementing strategy, not only to secure the rights for children of minority groups, but for all children who have been denied their rights. Edelman was the leader of a coalition working for federal child-development legislation and the chief architect for the Comprehensive Child Development Act passed by the Congress in 1971.*

At the time of the interview she was busy planning the role of the Children's Defense Fund of the Washington Research

Project, which she founded in 1971, in designing new legislation, in monitoring the enforcement of existing laws, and in carrying out advocacy litigation in behalf of American children who are without the education, health, and welfare assistance they are entitled to receive.

Kids have been outside the political process and they've not had the kind of systematic advocacy that's required of any group in this country that's going to have any chance of anything.

I had always thought that basic lack of fairness—having been southern and black—that suspension and expulsions were a process in the aftermath of school desegregation in the South. We've gone to Portland, Maine, and I just tell you—and we've gone to Cambridge and Somerville and little towns in Massachusetts and Iowa. And everything that's going on in Mississippi is going on in Portland, Maine. The distinction is that the people in Mississippi who are black are aware of it and are challenging it and they know they can do something about it and know it's bad. Parents in Portland, Maine, don't know they should have a hearing right for their kids, don't know that the school board's expelling and that there's something they can do about it. In the middle class it's called dyslexia and they all have special programs. But poor folk are called mentally retarded or dumb.

What's been striking to me is how far behind white parents are about their schools, about their problems. People have come back in tears every day out of Somerville, Massachusetts, which is a largely all-white suburb in the city here that's just a sewerage. I mean, it's unbelievable. The number of white children we have found who simply cannot read is astonishing. I mean, it's astonishing. We've been suing Canton, Mississippi, to desegregate for years but Winifred Green called me and said, "We've monitored for the first time the white community of Canton, Mississippi. I found three white children here today, under fifteen, who had not been to school in three years." She said, "The mother moved down here from another place. She asked the school board for transportation; the school board said 'no.' And it never occurred to them to contest it." Going through these kitchens with these lower classes—they just simply don't know that there's a problem that anybody can do anything about. Most whites still blame themselves and their children, though they are now beginning to hate the schools in the sense of "My kid's not reading, or my kid is treated badly." But they're still not sure it's not their fault. And even if they were convinced it's all the school's fault, they're not clear at all that they can do anything about it. And so there's just this hopelessness. And they all wanted to talk. I had thought they'd never let us in to come sit down but they did, and we sat there for hours in these kitchens with these white folk.

BENJAMIN SPOCK *I have known Benjamin Spock since the late 1930s when we were pediatricians at the New York Hospital-Cornell Medical Center, each dissatisfied with his training in the care and prevention of the emotional problems of children. Spock sought to help first by getting training in psychiatry and psychoanalysis; and, second, by writing professional articles for other pediatricians and writing books for parents on the care and rearing of children. Although he has become world famous as an author, he has participated in a variety of political activities because he believes real change to help America's children will only come through social change, which results from political action.*

We really should look at the contradictions of American society—we have more delinquents, more criminals, than we've ever had before and more than there's been in any other country, showing the sickness of our society. In trying to think back to why America is such a violent place, I assume that the people who came and settled here were rough-and-ready types; certainly they treated the Indians ruthlessly and treated subsequent waves of immigrants badly; and all the groups turned around and treated blacks badly. Then we developed this worship of rugged individualism, this attitude fostered by the industrial and business community that that is where our greatness is—in competition at all costs. Now on top of that we have television violence, which I used to minimize, laugh off as a corrupting or brutalizing influence, but I've changed my mind completely on that.

I used to assume that we were a child-centered society. Some of the things that made me wonder and then change my mind were hearing sensitive American women who'd lived abroad for several years come back to America and say that the thing that shocked them most was the abuse of children in the United States—children being hit in public, children being yanked along the street, children being yelled at constantly. I was impressed with it myself a year and a half ago in going to China and seeing how politely children are dealt with. In the fifteen days we were in China doing nothing but looking at children, children in groups, children on the streets, only once did I ever see an old grandmother make a motion as if pretending to swat a boy who was being a little obstreperous in the street. But in all the homes, in all the schools, and all the hospitals, children being treated so politely again made me realize we may be child-centered in one sense, but certainly there is a large proportion of Americans who take out all their resentments and their hostility—and there's a lot of resentment and hostility in the United States—on their children.

We're obviously deliberately neglecting poor families, neglecting poor children, because there's such an overwhelming spirit of "let's each of us take care of ourselves and get ahead and the devil take the hindmost."

SHELDON WHITE *After a long period of training and experience in different areas of psychology, White became a teacher and researcher at Harvard, where he is professor of psychology. He directed the review of the federal programs which were established in the 1960s for the benefit of disadvantaged young children. The resulting study, published in 1973, reviewed data about child development and evaluation of programs for children. The final report set forth recommendations for federal program planning, and White established himself as a competent critic within the field of child development. In addition, he has stimulated colleagues to view their work in the context of social policy and political activity. Another noteworthy contribution of his is "Human Research and Human Affairs," a paper presented at a symposium on "The Developmental Sciences: State and Fate of Research Funding," AAAS, Chicago, December 1970.*

I believe that . . . forces of modern life have combined (1) to attack the family—that is, to make families less secure and less able to take care of kids; (2) to provide no social place for children until they are twenty-five years of age; and (3) to . . . create a distinct shortage of social place for many adults. I think families are in tough shape because they are living in cities and because they are not living in housing that's designed for family life. They have to, because of our complex society, share their control over their children with a bureaucracy of whole-child professionals and any bureaucracy makes mistakes. So, families are, in fact, in a lot of trouble because the families love the kids and the kids love the families and yet, families cannot manage the destiny of children as they once did.

We are in a problem of social design. I believe that at the turn of the century we changed our social contracts; we asserted children's rights, but more than that, we asserted a system in which there was forever after to be division of labor between the family and teachers, pediatricians, reading specialists—a whole group of professional people who had to coordinate their activities with each other and with the family. We basically gave to society part of the responsibility for child rearing. We haven't to this day decided where religion belongs, whether it belongs in the family or the school, and we are a little messed up about sex education—we don't know whether that should be at home or in the school. But we bureaucratized and we professionalized and we monetized the care of children. And because children are delicate and precious commodities it's much more agonizing for them than for the adults to face shortcomings in the bureaucratic process. It's comical when an adult gets messed up in the Army but it's not comical when a child gets messed up in school.

I think we've got a second problem. At the turn of the century—I have seen data on this—if a kid was retarded, not badly (familially retarded), he didn't have a bad future. He could grow up and he could get a place in the economy. He could live pretty well. He wouldn't be distinguished, wouldn't be a great man, but a person with an IQ of 70 could make it in our society. If a kid has an IQ of 70 nowadays, that's catastrophic. I believe automation has been hitting us seriously since the turn of the century, at least. And because of automation we have progressively pushed the aged, children, and by malicious assignment, minorities, out of work. I heard a talk by Willard Wirtz last year; he argued that basically most children between sixteen and twenty-five are unemployed in our society no matter what it looks like they are doing. Those who are employed between sixteen and nineteen are basically in go-nowhere jobs. Those who are neither unemployed nor in those jobs are in college and I would argue that is for many of them a form of unemployment. We've lost a place in society for children until age twenty-five . . . and we've got a bunch of people who have nothing to do. One of the problems with educational reform—the reason we keep screaming about it and never do it—is, in part, that a great deal of education is not serious. It is warehousing. If you were to try and reform education you'd have to separate the day care and the warehousing. An awful lot of education is just basically finding places for kids who can't work.

URIE BRONFENBRENNER   *Known familiarly as Urie to countless persons, ranging from university students and academic colleagues to staff members of philanthropic foundations and congressmen, Urie Bronfenbrenner is an advocate for children wherever he believes he may influence changes in policy and programs. When I interviewed Senator Walter Mondale and Congressman Albert Quie, they cited Bronfenbrenner as the ideal type of academician to educate politicians about child development and to advise them concerning legislation to benefit families and children. Bronfenbrenner sees children developing in relationship to a variety of persons, places, and experiences, and considers that the most important primary influence, along with biological factors, is that of the family.*

Bronfenbrenner no longer holds to a simple "child-centered approach," but supports a broader "family-centered, community-centered, neighborhood approach because there is no way of facilitating the development of a child except through systems in which he has to grow." Currently professor of human development and family studies and of psychology at Cornell University, Bronfenbrenner has written many papers, articles, and books, and edited several anthologies on the development of human behavior. A good sample of both his wide-ranging and special interests in this field appears in his anthology Influences on Human Development.

How do you create support systems which enable families to function? In our contemporary American society these systems are falling apart and . . . it is getting increasingly difficult for parents to behave as parents. One of the things I can be proud of, I suppose, is that ten years ago I was saying in the National Advisory Council: "We are getting into a situation where we will have increasing child abuse, increasing child neglect. These processes are breaking down. We have to do something about them. We're going to get an alienation, we're going to get all this kind of thing. We must do something." Because this is the way it seemed to me the thing was moving. I have the unhappy satisfaction of now seeing that development occur.

Industry as it is now organized in terms of mobility, in terms of how you don't live near your work, in terms of the obligations you have that aren't counted as working time . . . creates a situation in which there is no time to be a parent.

We have allowed technology to dehumanize us . . . because we have allowed it to create situations which segregate ages and segregate sexes and segregate people on the basis of income and all the rest of it. It's particularly important in terms of segregation by age because as a result children do not see any role models older or younger. They don't learn how to deal with older or younger people than themselves and without that opportunity the whole process of socialization breaks down.

The problem is going to get worse before it gets better. Children's problems, such as drugs, alienation, the dropout, the child abuse—all of these things, I think, until we do something—are just going to keep growing like cancers.

ELIZABETH WICKENDEN *Although Elizabeth Wickenden served as an advisor to Presidents Roosevelt, Kennedy, and Johnson and as a staff member in several federal agencies and commissions, her knowledge of politics and of social and public policy-making has been equaled by her genuine concern for the well-being of families and children.*

Her goals have been to overcome such impediments to full developments of all persons as poverty, sickness, and inadequate housing and nutrition through design of social policy, federal legislation, and its adequate implementation, as well as through the work of voluntary private organizations.

She is a compassionate, pragmatic social planner, with strong belief in the role of the family in fostering individual development, but she recognizes the need of community support to sustain it. Wickenden was formerly professor of urban studies in the Graduate School and University Center of the City University of New York, and currently serves as consultant to the National Assembly of National Voluntary Health and Social Welfare Organizations.

One of her most provocative papers, "Today's Children: Our Debt to the Future," was read at the 1972 Conference of Executives of the Child Welfare League of America on November 20, 1972, in Chicago, Illinois.

People say to me sometimes, "How come that we had so much child care available during the war?" Well, it's a very simple matter. We absolutely had to have the labor of those women, and therefore we were prepared to pay for day care as part of the price for winning the war. Nowadays, the day-care enthusiasm on the part of Congress has been the by-product of a desire to save money and also a disapproval of women at home. Members of Congress, most of whom have never raised children and have never had experience with what it means to take care of children in congregate care, imagine to themselves, "Well, we've got fifty women on ADC; we can take two of these women and let them take care of the children of all the rest and that way we'll be getting a 48:2 cost-benefit ratio. It has never worked out that way. It never will work out that way. But it is a by-product of a dissatisfaction with very large public assistance rolls.

The Puritan work ethic applies particularly . . . when it comes, unfortunately, to black women. Senator Long, who is chairman of the committee that handles public assistance in the Senate said, at the time Elliot Richardson was up for confirmation: "Mr. Richardson, I don't care about your qualifications. What I want to know is are you going to find me somebody to wash my shirts?" He had in the back of his mind that black women with children went out to do laundry or took it home. And there is unfortunately strong prejudice which operates against the marginal population—in some areas it's black and in some areas it's Puerto Rican or Chicano or Indian or maybe mountain white in the mountain states. But these people are a different class of people which should be held to a different standard of performance than one thinks of for oneself.

We have beavers in our pond come every spring. Every year the Conservation Commission of New York State comes and removes the beavers to what is considered a safe spot. I'd say that if we spent half as much attention on our children as we do our beavers we'd be doing a lot better job. It's really a question of values. If we wanted to do these things we could do them precisely as they are done in Scandinavian countries and in others. So far, we have not come to place the value on children that we do on private consumption, having two cars, or other private benefits. I think that our basic philosophy is lacking. I picked up a quotation from an anthropologist named Earl E. Counts in which he said that the way you could distinguish the human creature from the anthropoid ape was the point at which the human child became the concern of the whole community and not the concern of a single mother. Well, if that's the definition of the human race we haven't gotten very far because we do not have this sense. In very primitive societies you have a far more universal—within the limits of the small community—responsibility toward all children than we, in our complex society, have toward all children. I spent a year in Iran, and there were very severe earthquakes there with thousands of people killed and rendered homeless. The shah and the queen sent out agents to try and pick up the orphaned children. There were no orphaned children because the community had gathered round these children and every child was attached to someone, either a relative or some member of the community. We do not have that sense of common responsibility.

I should say one or two things about the Nixon administration, because what has happened now is that the whole field of social welfare—and I think the same goes for other forms of public services including public health—has tended to be denigrated or discredited. And so, no longer is it possible to say that child welfare is honored and ADC is not honored. They're none of them honored. And I feel that we are going to have to rebuild public support almost from small beginnings. The natural concern of people for children has to be the nucleus on which we rebuild our public structure. There has been a tendency to fragment, to limit, the federal responsibility to the concept of revenue-sharing and to downgrade all professional input. Social workers have virtually disappeared from the federal agencies. The present head of the principal social welfare unit, the Social and Rehabilitation Services, is a certified public accountant. The social welfare field has been so far discredited that it is now treated as a management problem. The idea that the child is important in and of itself is simply not there. Day care is seen as a way of allowing the mother to work, rather than as a means of enlarging the child's experience. And this is part of our overall national crisis.

I think one of the reasons that we have so much family breakdown among poorer people is that we are now putting an impossible burden on the nuclear family, both the father and the mother. We no longer have the surrounding large family, we no longer have the small community supportive of the family, and we have not created organized institutions to perform the functions that were formerly performed by the large family. Take the mother of young children who works typically maybe a 16-hour day, and nobody thinks she should have a vacation from those children. We need to make life more tolerable for that mother and indirectly for that father. We have, I forget the number of millions of working fathers who are working as hard as they can, sometimes even at more than one job, who cannot raise their families, their children, above what we acknowledge to be the poverty line. Until we put more community support under these families they will continue oftentimes to do a rather poor job. I think the real heroine in all this is the deserted Negro mother. I think that, far from being the butt of total disapproval, these black women who have somehow fought and struggled for their children are the true heroines of their times. But I would like to see enough support there that their men don't feel the necessity of leaving them. There was a wonderful movie called "Nothing But a Man" of a Negro father trying to stick with his family under the most adverse conditions.

But this is simply one aspect of a much larger thing. I think people in our peculiarly disoriented era are suffering agonies of loneliness, that a mother with her family is lonely for larger support and that this in turn reflects itself on the children in a feeling of deprivation. I think one has to start with the assumption that some things are not measurable; you can't have a social indicator that measures loneliness. Subjective feelings are not, by any science yet developed, measurable, and I personally think they will never be subject to quantitative measurement.

LEE SALK

Lee Salk is a psychologist who teaches pediatricians to think of children as behaving, feeling, thinking beings, not only when they are sick or in trouble, but when they are healthy and coping satisfactorily in their family, their school, and their social relations. He is also a popular writer of books and articles for parents on child development and rearing. As such, he is rapidly attaining the influence and status among laymen long enjoyed by Benjamin Spock. Thus his ideas about the state of children today, the place of the modern family, women's liberation, and the role of the parent educator are of great value. Salk is professor of psychology in pediatrics and psychiatry at the New York Hospital-Cornell University Medical Center, and a member of the pediatrics department at the Lenox Hill Hospital in New York City.

My analysis of the problem is that professionals have never shown great recognition of children. Professionals in industry, in government, have shown no recognition of the family. When funds are cut, the first funds that are cut are concerning children's needs—in particular, children's health needs. It is rather amazing that we are regarded, at times, as a child-oriented society. I think that is a myth. We are not. Children don't vote, consequently politicians don't focus their interest on children. I think that professionals like you and professionals like myself have not done enough to speak up on behalf of parenthood. The people who do parent education have rarely been the professors or the people of the highest academic credentials. If you look at the procedures used in a hospital during childbirth, you see that, oftentimes, they try to separate the family—keep the father away from the delivery room, prevent the little brothers and sisters from coming to visit the mother and see the new baby—all for the convenience of the professional and not to support the integrity of the family. The women's movement has been attacked for having caused the destruction of the family, and I do not believe that at all. In fact, I think the women's movement has served a very, very important function. I think it has led to progress; it has led more people to consider what's happening in their lives. It's the women's movement that is pressing for flexible working hours for parents. They are pushing for the idea that fathers should be more involved in child-rearing.

I think the people who have been blaming the women's movement—industry and government—for having destroyed the family are really the culprits. I have seen many, many children with emotional problems who have never had a chance to see their fathers because fathers are sent off on business trips all the time, and industry won't pay for travel for the family. Or when the family is uprooted from New York and sent to St. Louis or from St. Louis to some other place, the children never get a chance to make an adjustment in school and the wives are prevented from having any kind of substantial socialization and are ruptured from other relatives. I think this is what caused the dissolution. Let me put it another way. I don't think that's caused the dissolution of the family; it's the attitude about the family . . . which has caused the dissolution of the family. If they respected the needs of the family more they would never have done those things, but it's the attitude that is far more important. I wish we could make government and industry recognize that the family needs are of equal importance—in my own mind, even more important—to the occupational needs.

WILLIAM KESSEN *As his colleague at Yale, I witnessed William Kessen's maturation from able graduate student in psychology to articulate scholar in the field of child development. As befits one of his sensitivity, he is critical of his profession and of those like himself who (although often at the cost of internal conflict) continue to enjoy the aesthetic pleasure afforded by carefully controlled laboratory research even though they are aware of the existence of perplexing problems which demand study now because they threaten the well-being, even the lives, of so many children. Kessen is professor of psychology at Yale University and the author of many articles and books on child development. His latest contribution is his compilation of papers prepared by a team of social scientists who visited China under his leadership, which has been published as* Childhood in China.

We have protected children from common diseases, and increasingly protected infants. Again, one can fuss because we haven't done as much as one might. But over the historical haul there's just no doubt about that. We have made their development more likely and more interesting by the availability of materials, which has been a marvelous and dramatic change over the last hundred years. The display of *things* is so much more great and interesting for children.

It seems to me that where we have not done as well as we might—where, as a matter of fact, we may have gone backwards—is in putting on them . . . such enormous achievement requirements. The whole notion of being "successful" almost at any cost has meant that development within institutions, particularly within schools, has very little to do with human enlargement but with ways of getting to the next step. So that in quite a fundamental way the function of the second grade is to get to the third and that kind of regularity of institutional development seems to me to be most unfortunate. Aside from this institutional demand for achievement . . . is the narrowing of interactional patterns. To put it in the most exaggerated way, a child knows fourteen adults by the time he is twenty-one: two parents and twelve school teachers. And I think it is most unfortunate. I don't think it's solved by trips to the farm or museums. I really think it means a secular change and probably an irreversible change in the culture.

LOLA NASH

Lola Nash is director of the Edith B. Jackson Child Care Program and lecturer at the Yale Child Study Center. When interviewed she was director of a day-care center in New Haven for children of poor people, most of whom were black. As such she is faced with the difficult task of hundreds of others who receive public monies for the support of a day-care center, that of justifying her work with quantified evidence obtained by instruments and methods which are too imprecise to provide the type of measurements demanded and where the objects to be assessed are highly idiosyncratic human characteristics, or abstract and ill-defined concepts.

One of the greatest difficulties the American child faces is that there are so many people who are saying what's good for the American child and yet they are in such conflict with each other. And I am not sure that anybody really has a clear picture. There are groups of people who feel very strongly that we must develop the child cognitively and that the cranial part of a child is the only necessary part of a child. So you have a proliferation of the kits—the kind of kits which carry out a whole behavioral approach. I think behaviorism has certainly overtaken the field of child development as well as many other fields in America. These kits are for parents, they are kits for teachers.

I went to a NAEYC conference in Washington this past November and I laughingly said to two of my colleagues: "We really ought to write an educational "Upstairs, Downstairs." *Upstairs,* in the lecture hall, was Dr. Kagan and all of the other educators telling us how we must deal with the total child, we must respect the child's feelings, and, most important of all, we must see an integration, a synthesis, between all aspects of what we are trying to do with children. *Downstairs* there was a huge hall which was filled with the commercial people selling things, and there were kits on how to make a child feel better, or worse, on how to make a child perform better, or worse, on how to make a child jump, scream, sing, dance, be creative, not be creative, learn the three Rs, not learn the three Rs. It's all programmed, and it is with as little "input" involvement, creativity, on the part of the adult and the teacher as possible.

And we begin to get the computer language as part of this: "What are our behavioral objectives?" "What is our time-flow chart?" "What is our time frame?" This is the way a lot of the material that comes through from Head Start begins to look. What we are being asked to do in terms of evaluation is all that we can write down in terms of objectives that are measurable. And I don't know how I can measure most of what we do here at the day-care center. So that is what really troubles me.

I think, too, that those who have children or deal with children who are less sophisticated, who are less educated, are taken in by all of this. It's tantalizing, it's seductive, and they are frightened that perhaps they don't know as much as the professionals, and so it's much safer to respond to something which is programmed than to think for one's self, to behave in a spontaneous way, to follow one's own intuition about the way one reacts to children. . . . I find "Sesame Street" one of the most destructive things that has happened, even though there are some good things in it and some fine people involved. But the total result is again one of *"This* child does so well," and therefore the child who doesn't in some way is looked at in a less respected way.

STEPHEN HESS *Stephen Hess, a political scientist, was chosen by President Richard Nixon to organize the 1970 White House Conference. He is now senior fellow in the Governmental Studies Program of the Brookings Institution.*

We pay lip service to the child but where are the results? If you look at the way the government spends its money in some sort of breakdown by age, children receive a very small percentage compared, for example, to the aging. I don't think it will change soon, in part because children can't vote and aren't organized and their lobbyists haven't learned to be effective.

LEON EISENBERG *Leon Eisenberg is an unorthodox child psychiatrist who exposes the deficiencies of psychiatric services, as well as deficiencies of our society which play an important role in the genesis of human suffering and ill health.*

His disillusionment with psychiatry, especially Freudian analysis, and with his psychiatric colleagues, so many of whom show no interest in the social and economic issues, inclines him to view pediatricians as the physicians who are best informed and have the more natural role in the alleviation and prevention of problems of mental health. Presently he is professor of psychiatry, Harvard Medical School, and senior associate in psychiatry, Boston Children's Hospital.

Both pediatrician and child psychiatrist have a major role to play in the area of child abuse. Study and understanding of the families that abuse children is a task for both. The problem, however, of child neglect, which is several orders of magnitude higher in the United States, is a problem that transcends simple parental inadequacies but that goes on to society's failures. You know, for the past ten years, a number of people working actively in the field of child nutrition have provided fairly strong, though not yet totally convincing, evidence that malnutrition afflicting the mother in the last trimester of pregnancy, or the infant in the first year or year and a half of life, may very well, if severe, result in irreversible brain stunting. We still don't feed children. But . . . let's say that the findings are wrong scientifically. Let's say that brain stunting can be reversed by adequate nutrition later. Does that mean children shouldn't be fed? Isn't it enough to argue on moral grounds that in this world there is no excuse for any child going hungry? Now, I think that is a moral problem our society generally has to face. I think professionals who see in their own work the consequences of hunger, and hunger not only for food but hunger for intellectual stimulation, hunger for affection, have a special responsibility to get out on the hustings and cry out to their fellow citizens that something must be done.

SIBYLLE ESCALONA *Sibylle Escalona is a well-known developmental psychologist, whose special field is the behavior of children.*

As a child she was observed as a research subject by a family friend, Kurt Lewin, a man who became the model of the ideal researcher for many students in child psychology. Like Lewin, Escalona also has an interest in society, its institutions and organizations, and their roles in child behavior. Presently, she is professor of psychology at the Albert Einstein College of Medicine in New York City. Her book The Roots of Individuality: Normal Patterns of Development in Infancy *testifies to her careful work as a researcher.*

If you wish to make a comparison among the major nations of the world, we are not devoting anywhere near the social effort or money to children as do a good many other countries. It seems to me that a great deal of the public effort, even that supposedly relating to children, is totally un-child focused. I think the enormous, what would seem to me to be overemphasis on stimulating cognitive development in very early childhood really has its origins in the social distress that arises with massive failure in school, with massive failures in adaptation in society on the part of young people. . . . I'm not talking about the motivation of individuals who engage in this work, but on a social level I think it is motivated by efforts to improve society, make people manipulable, preserve stability, and preserve the status quo in the, I think, mistaken hope that if you get them young enough you can make 'em behave more the way you'd like 'em to behave.

TOM LEVIN *Tom Levin has found his greatest satisfaction in combining his practice of psychology with his work and interest in the civil rights movement and in community organizations. He was formerly assistant professor of psychiatry and assistant professor of community health, Albert Einstein College of Medicine.*

Levin was one of the few social scientists who joined the movement in the 1960s in the South, where his greatest single achievement was the founding of a Head Start program called the Child Development Group of Mississippi. The story of that organization has become a document of historical importance for social scientists, students of government, educators of young children, and citizens involved in community change.

Always articulate, Levin speaks frankly and critically of society, the child-development movement, the roles of women, and the problems of children. He feels that there is an urgent need for changing those conditions and circumstances that hinder development of children's full potential. At the present time he has a private practice in psychotherapy.

The child-welfare movement was a response to a social need. It wasn't to raise children in a better way. It's that our society could not tolerate children wandering around—when its affluence developed—and dying, and impinging on our conscience. The same way that the health movement developed in

America; it developed out of social need, not out of having any humanism. There are very good reasons why. If you let kids wander around that way you are educating a group of asocial and antisocial citizens who will disrupt society. So you have to do something. If you don't have free clinics and hospitalization in an urban setting where you have industrialization, you have plague, and plague kills middle class as well as poor, and it destroys workers. It is a social force. We delude ourselves that it's humanism. We have to get in touch with the social forces. In some ways that is cruel. It strips us of our illusions, but that is what we have to do.

At present the child-development movement is not a child-development movement. That's bullshit. The child-development people are trying to put child-development inputs into it, and I think they should try. It is a social-change movement; it has to do with the changing role of men and women in our society, the changing definition of what the relationship between self function and work function is. I would say there is a *human*-development movement in this country. One of the facets of it is the total rethinking of family structure and we're beginning to deal with the politics of families and how this effects social policy.

People like R. D. Laing, in an abstract way, talk about it. The communes live it. Perhaps the avant-grade, the flying wedge, are ADC mothers who say, "Look, I don't accept your definition of family. I want children; I don't have a husband." It's a particular kind of thrust. The new movement, the new wedge, is now the women's liberation movements which are demanding a realignment of traditional functions—social functions which were then precipitated into family politics. Family politics had to do with mother as a nurturant force of the children. She carried the social values. Father passed on those values to mother and supported the mother. That's changing.

I think it's going to be a twenty-five-year development in which essentially we're going to find in the end that we're going to change our whole social concept of raising children from that of a family responsibility to that of a community responsibility. I think that's the overall trend. And in this we go through lots of different things. Middle-class families, which have more supports built in, will hold on to the family concept longer. In many ways, the upper class and the lower class have always gone much faster toward its being a social responsibility. The upper-class children are not raised by their parents; they're raised according to certain social values which are imparted by delegated authority. The lower classes, the under classes, are into that, too. The middle class will move last.

WILLIAM M. SCHMIDT *Trained in pediatrics and public health, William Schmidt is a physician who has worked in a variety of agencies and institutions responsible for providing health care to children, including the U.S. Children's Bureau, the American Joint Distribution Committee in Paris, and the U.S. Office of Foreign Relief and Rehabilitation Operations. In 1974 he retired as professor of maternal and child health, Harvard School of Public Health.*

The salient problem affecting children today [is] inequality. A given level of health or lack of health or mortality rate, or whatever it is, really gains in significance by comparison. There are no absolutes in this field. People are not absolutely healthy or they're not absolutely non-healthy. Everybody's betwixt and between, really. And the question is then, "How do I stack up with other people?" I think that's what most people tend to feel. Now, if a person feels, "It's hard. I am not very well. I need a lot of attention, but other people do too, and what attention they're getting I'm getting," it is easier to bear, it seems to me. And people are less upset and less cast down. For example, many people say, "Well, look at the blacks. How much they've improved. Look at their infant mortality rate, their maternal mortality rate and how they have fallen in these years from very high levels to very low levels." True, but whereas a generation ago the black maternal mortality rate was twice as high as the white (for example) it's now about four times as high as the white. So that while they've improved greatly compared to their own past, which is important, they've really not improved or even gotten a little bit behind the parade still farther in comparison with the whites. Now I think this affects people adversely; I think it affects both the blacks and the whites adversely.

When I was in the Children's Bureau in the Labor Department and reading all the books they had around there, I ran into Frederick Douglass's book, *My Life as a Freedman and as a Slave,* and in it he said that slavery was an institution that hurt the slaveholder as well as the slave. Now, I had never thought about that before. And I think that the effect of inequality is that. It blunts the finer feelings of people who profit from inequality. And, of course, I think that there are other ill-effects. I think that the children who consume excessively, who are protected excessively—let's say from the penalties of delinquency (they commit a bad offense but they can be protected)—are hurt in a different way.

I'm saying that the inequality of care, of concern, of treatment are bad on both sides. So, looking back at the years I've had at Harvard, I think that one of the things that our department has done has been to open this kind of question with students again and again and again. Our department has tended to try to focus the students' attention on the human values and human issues involved in programs of health care. There's been an increasing tendency to talk about efficiency, cost effectiveness, cost benefits, careful selection of priorities. You have to be able to prove that a given service will have a defined, measurable, quantitative benefit, like reducing the infant mortality a few points. Benefits such as leading to greater comfort are not as easily measurable, so they're not in there. Or benefits leading to a sense of self-worth or of satisfaction ("This was a good experience," sort of thing) don't get measured so easily.

EDWARD ZIGLER *This respected scholar of child psychology, who has a special interest in the educability of the mentally retarded child, left his position in the academic world for a temporary one in government. As the first full-time director of the Office of Child Development, he soon learned the intricate workings of a bureaucracy, as well as the special characteristics of the Nixon administration. As an administrator of a new federal agency with responsibilities to both his superiors in the government and to the people the agency served, he noted many contrasts between his new role and his former one as a protected scholar in academia.*

He left OCD with new awareness of the plight of America's children, resolved to modify his own academic career in order to communicate not only with peers but also with the nonprofessional persons who carry the largest responsibility for providing opportunities for children and family development. Zigler is professor of psychology at the Yale Child Study Center and the Institution for Social and Policy Studies. He has written extensively on the education of mentally retarded children.

My own efforts in Washington, prior to going there full time . . . convinced me that much of what we do for children in this country, much legislation, much administration and programs, are actually outcome products of the efforts of individuals who are not terribly knowledgeable about children or what makes them tick, which is rather sad. There hasn't been the ability. There have been some exceptions but, by and large, children's programs are in the hands of bureaucrats who might as well be at the post office.

Until there is a real awareness in this nation of the shortfalls of this country in respect to what we do for children, until there is a national dialogue, until there's a real sense that something is wrong and something should be done by the person in the street, I think very little is going to be done, because the myth is still abroad in the land that this is a child-oriented society—nothing is too good for our children and they need nothing. Well, at the same time we have children who are hungry and . . . a million and a half children who are latchkey children who don't have proper supervision or care.

WILLIAM SMITH *William Smith served first as counsel to Senator Joseph S. Clark and the Subcommittee on Employment and Manpower, then as counsel to the Select Committee on Nutrition and Human Needs chaired by Senator George McGovern, and finally as counsel to Senator Walter Mondale and the Select Committee on Equal Educational Opportunity.*

Smith's position with the Children's Defense Fund affords him the opportunity to plan litigation in behalf of children deprived of their health, education, and legal rights.

As a society and as a matter of public policy, we are not prepared to make the investment that we should make in the future of our children and I mean the distant future. It costs a lot less to educate a child when you think in terms of the long-term investment of that education and the fact the child is going someday to be a consumer of our gross national product and so forth. If you think in terms of long-term economic investment of education or whatever, or health care, or whatever it might be, the cost-benefit ratio is entirely different than if you think in terms of an investment in a program like Head Start and you look three years later and you try to figure out whether it worked or not. There are very few people that are willing to think, "What is this investment going to mean to us in terms of benefit thirty years from now, or twenty years from now, when that child becomes an adult?"

KENNETH KENISTON *The Carnegie Corporation of New York, which has a long history of granting funds for child-development research, the study of child education, and child-care services, considered the 1970s an appropriate time for a major effort in their support of such endeavors. As one consequence, the corporation established the Carnegie Council on Children and appointed Kenneth Keniston its director. Although a psychologist, he had never worked in the field of child psychology or development. It was purposely so arranged that neither director nor staff should have had such experience in order that their explorations of the field avoid parochialism.*

The interview with Keniston took place near the designated end of the council's research and field work, when the writing of the final reports and recommendations had begun. Keniston's remarks, then, serve as a sort of distillate of his impressions of the history of child development and the measures that need to be taken now to deal with the plight of children.

Keniston is Mellon Professor of Human Development at the Massachusetts Institute of Technology. He is compiling a series of reports on the work of the Carnegie Council on Children that will be published in 1977.

We have now spent three years trying to define the problems of American children, trying to put our finger on some of the central problems and the peripheral problems. I don't think we have a final list or agreement, so I can only speak for myself. The way I am thinking about it at the moment is that we have a set of old problems that we have not solved—old promises that we have not kept to children. And then we have a set of new problems that are the result of the peculiar kind of technological society we live in.

It seems to me that one of the basic promises of this country was that everyone would be a full citizen of the society, and a further promise to parents was that even if they were in some sense excluded their children would have a chance of "making it," of joining the mainstreams of the society. Our work suggests that that promise is not kept for roughly 25 percent of all American children. These are, by and large, the children of very poor parents, of minority parents, children who are in some way handicapped, or children whose parents are so overwhelmed by life that they are unable to care for the children themselves. We are very fond of talking about the success stories, about the poor boys or girls who "made it" and about the handicapped people who did wonderful things and about the neglected children who became creative adults. But my sense of it is that those success stories are very exceptional and that there are millions and millions of American children who are born with three strikes against them.

It takes extraordinary parents, or extraordinary genius, or terribly good luck for their children to "make it." You are familiar with the catalogue—bad prenatal care, high risk at birth, birth defects, illnesses during childhood not taken care of, the stigmatization that goes with being a nonwhite minority, the enormous problems of poverty that affect, as you know, children in the poorest group in the country—a third of them with below the minimum decent income as reckoned by the Department of Labor—bad schools or inadequate schools, the failure to treat remedial defects in the earlier years of life. The devastating fact is that these damages to children usually occur in packages; they congregate. No one of them perhaps is enough to irreparably blight a child's chances but they accumulate. All these harms accumulate on one sector of society. So if you were to pick out the greatest national shame as far as children go, it's our failure really to think systematically about how we could include those children, how we could give them the kind of a chance that we have been promising children since the beginning of the first white settlements on this land.

The other thing that I have become very impressed with is how terribly rapidly the lives of children and families and communities have changed in this country even in the past quarter of a century. I think we have not begun to realize what's happening to children and families at this point. This is in a sense a new problem. The rapidity of change since the Second World War is really staggering. Some of the figures that Urie Bronfenbrenner has been collecting, I think, demonstrate very clearly that the family has really been emptied of people—there are more mothers in the work force, a staggering increase in the single parent families mostly as a result of divorce, one out of every eight births is illegitimate at the present time, an enormous increase, the number of siblings drastically down. These trends have increased so rapidly and so dramatically that I think our image of American families has not caught up with the reality at all. Children are not in the presence of parents or other relatives—be they siblings or grandparents, or uncles—for an increasing amount of each day; more and more children come home to a house with no grown-ups in it. The care of children is more and more relegated to outsiders, nonfamily members; peer groups play an ever more important role in the socialization of children; and the television set has become a kind of ersatz parent.

I don't want to argue that the number of hours you spend in the presence of a child determines the quality of the interaction. There is no evidence that working mothers per se have any harmful effect on their children. But I think we run the danger of children being brought up, socialized, or whatever the word is—reared—more and more by their peers, by impersonal institutions, or by television, and less and less by their family members. I think we know that children need the kind of very exquisite, unconscious responsiveness that continuous caretakers develop. They also develop that kind of responsiveness to their caretakers. There is a kind of accommodation of the child's needs and the caretaker's needs. I think we also know that, by and large, it is more likely to occur in a family situation than in most other situations.

Another new problem I see is the enormous emphasis on the child as a brain—that is, the focus on reading scores, IQ tests, cognitive development. All of this is fine, but it is increasingly emphasized today to the exclusion of human care and compassion, moral sensibility and altruism and all of the other kinds of human qualities that matter a lot more than an IQ. And I think that runs very much through the school system and through our whole society and affects children profoundly and I would think adversely.

Still another trend that is affecting children, that has a long history but is culminating now, is the virtual disappearance of organic communities in this country. They have been slowly disappearing for two centuries, until at the present time I think most Americans live in neighborhoods where at best there are friendly strangers. We are forced as a people to turn to paid professional assistance as the first line of help. Ideally, I think we would turn to our friends, our neighbors, to community resources, in an informal way first and only then, if that didn't work, to backup professional and paid expert services.

Behind a lot of this, I think, lies . . . a very high-powered modern technological economy in which innovation, consumption, expansion and growth-profit are very central. There is a real fusion between the economic and the political sectors of our society, so that to attack the American economy and the way it's run is almost like attacking the country or the government. To simplify greatly, in many cases the needs of the building industry, or the food industry, or the toy industry, or the television industry, or the housing industry, take precedence over any assessment of human and social needs, for families with children in particular. We don't build communities; we build houses in rows. We worry about fire codes but we never stop to think about community facilities and how the man-made environment could encourage people to interact, to help each other. The pressures that are pushing women into the labor force are largely economic pressures, but we rarely ask whether there are other ways of supporting family income, particularly for those many women who would prefer not to have to work when their children are young.

Also at work here is a very powerful value system, the latter-day incarnation of the American work ethic. For 150 years, since the time of Andrew Jackson, we have defined children as valuable insofar as they were going to be productive members of the economy. I think if there is one central stand in our definition of a "good child," it's a child who will be productive, but productive not in a sense of creative, imaginative, and so forth, but productive in the sense of earning a good living, contributing to the economy. And as our society becomes more technological and more oriented toward knowledge, the productive child is a child who uses its head, the child who does well on tests, who can pass the various hurdles to get through the schools, and go to college and get a good degree and get a good job.

We really began from a question that Al Solnit asked, "Why don't Americans like children?" In the end I concluded that this is not quite the right way to put it. As individuals, American parents do care for their children, do their best by them, love them; it is not that we as a nation have some particular hatred of children. I think the explanation lies in the way we separate our own children from other people's children and the way in which the kind of individualism of American society, kind of competitive individualism, the fear of dependency, economic dependency in particular, then justifies or legitimizes or even encourages us not to be concerned with other people's children. If, after all, you believe that we are all on our own and that it is for the best if everybody competes, then that absolves you of any responsibility, or undercuts your feeling of concern, for other children. If you further believe, as I think Americans tend to, that to help people is in some way to weaken and enfeeble them—so they will become dependent, or they will become paupers, or they will become welfare cases—then that is a further impediment to acting out of any natural instinct of generosity and responsibility. So, at the cultural level, the feeling of every man or woman for himself, coupled with the feeling that the family is a private preserve, a castle that nobody comes in without permission, added to the feeling that to assist people is to make them dependent and weak—all these feelings conspire against those feelings of concern and generosity that we have, and in the end, prevent our concern from translating itself into public policy.

Another factor historically, that has prevented the assumption of any serious public responsibility for the next generation is the distinction—which again goes back 150 or more years—that we make between adequate and inadequate families. The adequate family in this country has been defined, by and large, as the self-sufficient family that needs no help. It's always been a myth because obviously every family has always needed help and especially so today. But visibly to need help still pushes a family into the condition of inadequacy. The price in America for getting help has been to admit one's inadequacy and to accept the stigma attached to public assistance. Just to think about that word is interesting. Public assistance suggests some kind of dole, and not help from one's community, which it might mean. To say that somebody is on "public assistance" is to say a very negative thing. So, the artificial segregation between the self-sufficient, autonomous, self-contained family on the one hand and on the other hand the inadequate, dependent, needy family has been another factor that has stood in the way of any across-the-board entitlement to *all* families that need help or support with services.

In the age of Jackson we devised two basic notions, first that this is a land of equal opportunity and, secondly, that schooling is the equalizing vehicle by which people will find their own deserved level. These are terrifically central doctrines in American life even today. The programs of the 1960s, for example, the war on poverty . . . ended up not with jobs or income redistribution, but with Head Start, which was premised on the notions of equal opportunity and of schooling. The problem with these notions is that they both happen to be incorrect; that is, opportunity is no greater in this country than in many others, and there is very little evidence that schooling per se equalizes people's chances. On the contrary, right now the privileged and the underprivileged get further and further apart the more schooling they have.

WALTER MONDALE

Vice-President Walter Mondale has become even more aware of the problems of children through hearing the testimony of parents, teachers, physicians, and psychologists. He readily agreed to an interview because he feels an obligation as a member of the Congress to press for social reform. He has become one of the most active advocates of children in planning and designing legislation and in arranging coalitions with other members of the Congress for bipartisan support of such measures as the Comprehensive Child Development Act of 1971.

Mondale is critical of those who impeded his efforts in congressional action. His predominant mood is one of cautious expectation of change and his determination to press for new legislative measures for children is undiminished.

The picture is not all black, of course. I would say that the majority of American children are brought up with good health care, strong families with resources available to do what's needed, opportunities for advanced education and other forms of fulfillment, and employment ahead of them—which is a very bright picture indeed for those children who are privileged to have that kind of environment in which to grow up. But, in my opinion, there is an absolutely inexcusable proportion of American children whose lives are entirely different. Some are in what you might call the poverty category, so denied in terms of the normal, and needed, cultural and environmental supports and health care and the rest—emotional support, assistance in educational and developmental processes—that their life expectations in terms of hope for sharing in American life are very dim indeed, and that becomes obvious even before they start school.

Added to that are the continuing problems of discrimination. I think it is still very difficult for a child who comes into this life in our country with a different color to expect an equal shot at the chances in our country. There are many other children who suffer burdens and barriers that they cannot handle themselves and their families can't handle who are not in the what you might call poverty class—at least as defined by the Bureau of Labor Statistics. These are the children with emotional problems, physical handicaps, and other kinds of difficulties that can only be handled with substantial investments of money and that money just isn't available. And, of course, there are many other needs; millions of kids, preschool and school age, whose parents are both working or whose only parent is working, are left largely unattended or in substandard day-care centers and the rest and don't receive the normal emotional and other kinds of help which other children do. Then, of course, you've got the problems of second-rate schools; usually the children I am talking about are offered only the second-rate schools. There are many other problems that have been detailed and well known and exclaimed and decried about for all these seventy-five years . . . and longer.

Now, we have done some modest things that are important: we do have Title I, Elementary and Secondary Education Act; we do have a handicapped program; we have an Office of Child Development; we have the child-abuse program; we have a children's health program; we have screening programs, and the rest. But I don't know of anyone who has studied this field who thinks those programs and their funding or the way in which they are administered in any way approximate the scope of the problem. And, of course, during much of my career in the Senate I have tried to develop the kind of political clout that we need to bring these programs up to what's needed. And that is one of the things that led . . . to the creation of the Subcommittee on Children and Youth where we have tried through a small staff and through hearings to try to listen to the range of problems which children have and then try to implement change through legislation and appropriation.

I think we have made some progress but, on the whole, it's been quite disappointing. Partly, I suppose, it's the times. I often think if we had done the same thing in the best years of Lyndon Johnson and John Kennedy, and before the war destroyed us, when there was a good mood of social reform and there was a sense of hope about giving people a chance, and we were generating growing resources because of a stable economy, that we might have been able to really generate programs and monies needed to make a substantial difference in the life chances of these children. Alas, that didn't happen. I think the mood and the spirit of the Great Society was America at its best—a little too optimistic but, as someone has said, "You don't accomplish anything in a society without optimism." But then, of course, the promise of all those programs was destroyed by the Vietnam war . . . and, in a sense, we are paying the price not only because the programs didn't get fully funded but because we are being asked to justify those programs as though they were fully implemented and failed. In fact, in most cases, they were never tried, so it is a cruel twist . . . and increases our burden as we try to deal with these problems. As a matter of fact, I hear a lot of young liberals coming in now, saying, "None of these programs work." *They* are not even buying them. None of these programs have been tried as far as I am concerned, to any substantial extent.

Nixon, of course, was an abomination, not only in his antagonism to dealing with these problems but also in the example he provided for the kids, which couldn't have been worse. And while Ford provides a much nicer example of a decent human being, if anything he is more conservative than Nixon—or maybe less political. In other words, Nixon, I think, would bend once in a while because it might hurt him politically not to do so; Ford's social budget, his education, his child development—all those budgets—have just been slaughtered, and so it is very hard to make progress with that kind of leadership. The day may come—I hope it will come—when we will have presidential leadership pushing for these programs, using the influence of the White House to gain public support, and then our country will be able to apply those resources.

I say, "I hope so," but the longer I am in politics the less I am certain of it. There is something about the politics of children we have yet to solve. Maybe it is very simple. A friend of mine, a very conservative one, once said, "You know, you should do more for old people and forget those kids; they can't vote." And maybe that's the answer. In any event, it is a fact that the rhetoric, the ideals that we pronounce in American society about our children, and the fundamental principles of fairness in American life which should say, "We will prohibit discrimination, we will not have quotas but we will give everyone the equipment they need to try to achieve equality in American society," are a long way from fulfillment.

If you give the Defense Department all of what they want, or even half of what they want each year, and if you say that the tax loopholes can remain untouched, and if you do the other things that we have been pressed to do recently, there isn't much money left for children. That's part of the problem. Part of it, I think, is the remoteness and the impersonality of the problem for most Americans. There is nothing in the life of upper- and upper-middle-class Americans that exposes them, in a personal way, so that they know the problems of Jennie and John, and so on, and not in terms of statistics—which are deadly.

SALLY PROVENCE *Beginning as a clinical pediatrician, Provence has become a foremost researcher of infant and young child behavior. She is a professor of pediatrics at the Yale University School of Medicine, and director of the child development unit of its Child Study Center.*

Her extensive research on the possibilities of positive inter-

vention in the lives of infants and young children seemingly doomed to pathology by their racial, social, and economic background qualifies her to speak as she does now.

What I am really increasingly concerned about . . . is I guess what I would condense under the rubric of the lack of adequate support systems for young parents in child-rearing. It seems to me that almost every place that I look I see, not just in our clinic here but elsewhere, the fact that young parents do not have the kind of tangible supports, or psychological supports, for parenthood while their children are young. I suspect this can only partially be supplied ever by professionals such as you and myself and others, and the problem then of how to supply this through some substitute for the old neighborhood, through some substitute for the extended family, is one of the foremost problems of our days as I see it. I am worried about it because I see the impact on the satisfaction of the parents but even more on the development of the children which seems to me to reflect the fact that they simply aren't being nurtured as well as I like to think they used to be. We have seen more children whose development is delayed in a variety of dimensions but we also have seen more children with disturbances in behavior and being difficult for their parents to manage, and getting into trouble with one another much earlier during the past ten years. I guess I would say we have seen many more disturbed youngsters of disturbed parents than was true of the ten years preceding.

Very few people in the mental-health professions have had a chance in their training in mental health, in psychiatry, in mental-health nursing, in social work, to have a firsthand experience with very young children. I just don't think you learn that from a book. So that our program, the training aspect of it, is really based on our conviction that if we can give these professionals a direct experience with parents and children when the children are very young, that they are going to be much more useful both as practitioners and as consultants to others. If we can't get mental-health professionals with that kind of knowledge of the early years, including the problems of early parenthood, into the primary health-care system somehow, I don't think our chances are very good of turning this situation around.

I can't quote the figures exactly but I have heard them recently—in training programs in child psychiatry there are fewer than 20 percent—I believe I am quoting it correctly—of the trainees who have a direct experience with children under five; it's a small percentage. With all the surface acceptance and lip service being paid to the importance of what happens in the early years, we don't yet act as if we believe in it very much, it seems to me.

2 Woe to the Parents Who Turn to the Experts

Advice on Child Rearing

1910—Spank them
1920—Deprive them
1930—Ignore them
1940—Reason with them
1950—Love them
1960—Spank them lovingly
1970—To hell with them?

> *A poster that appeared recently in a toy shop window.*

For at least a hundred years, parents have been showered with advice on how to rear their children. Ministers, educators, doctors, joined more recently by psychologists and psychiatrists and even politicians, have peddled their nostrums and often intimidated parents with threats of dire consequences if directions were not followed as given. As theories about the nature of children flourished, died, and were reborn in other guises, the counsel has undergone 180° shifts, which transformed the "good" practices of some decades into the unpardonable mistakes of others.

When the child-development movement got under way after World War I, the theories of John B. Watson, a behavioristic psychologist, were the vogue. Reflecting the postwar faith in science and convinced that the environment was virtually the sole determinant of how a child developed, Watson taught that practically anything could be accomplished with a child provided that the conditioning was appropriate. To establish good habits and sound discipline from the outset, he warned against maternal loving and cuddling and devised a rigid schedule, which was to be adhered to regardless of the infant's protests.

As Watson's influence declined in the thirties, hereditarian Arnold Gesell captured the attention of parents with his growth norms until the psychoanalytic theories of the Freuds, father Sigmund and daughter Anna, and their followers became the predominant influence in child-rearing, most notably through the writings of Benjamin Spock. Often, unfortunately, there were misinterpretations of Freudian concepts of development and hence misapplications. Along with other influences, these fostered the kind of "permissiveness" that was eventually exploited by the Nixon administration for all it was worth in votes. After the importance of Freudian concepts waned, the theories of cognitive development of Jean Piaget and his adherents occupied center stage in the 1960s and led to an emphasis on the importance of providing early learning experiences and stimulating environments for the very young child.

Today, a certain disillusionment with early learning as a

panacea has set in, the value of any "recipe" for child-rearing is being questioned, and the healthy idea is germinating that the feelings of parents about raising their children are due a certain measure of respect.

MILTON J. E. SENN

At the St. Louis Children's Hospital, with which I was associated in the early thirties, we were given no assistance or guidance in interviewing parents or in helping them in child-rearing practices. The emphasis in child-rearing was on an assumed scientific basis of strict scheduling of feeding and hours for sleeping and even for exposure to fresh air. Professor John Watson, a behaviorist leader in the field of American psychology, was read and his principles of child-rearing were followed regularly because they were considered based on scientific research. However, it was already apparent in the 1930s that mothers were beginning to doubt the correctness of the strict scheduling and were beginning to secretly feed the children when they were hungry, in amounts that seemed more adequate than those prescribed by the physician, and were even introducing foods at an earlier age than recommended by the doctors. When these mothers, usually with their second and third children, were able to "get away" with such practices with no seeming harm to the children and in fact with less crying and better sleeping patterns, word soon got around among the laity that doctors were overstrict and really unknowing of the needs of children.

However, because we were living in a scientific era of medical development, with great emphasis on carrying on research, sometimes done on animals and transferring the results to children, physicians felt uncomfortable in recommending a more permissive approach. As a consequence, mothers of firstborn tended to follow the hook and the physicians' recommendations strictly and then to accept the problems of feeding and sleeping as evidence of their failure as parents. When they came to the pediatrician with these problems, their feelings of guilt were increased by the doctor who tended to blame them for somehow making mistakes, not sticking strictly enough to the schedules prescribed, and to be actually punitive toward the mothers. When their recommendations continued to be met with failure, the physician in frustration and resentment put further blame on the mother and tried to spend less time with her because he felt that in this way he could protect himself from the complaints of an "overanxious" mother.

I am confused in understanding the acting-out of so many children today . . . and in understanding how much of this is related to permissiveness in child-rearing which Spock and I encouraged in infant feeding, toilet training, and disciplining. Certainly, I believe it is true that most people did not rear their children permissively in a healthy sense. Many times they deserted their children, neglected them, were ambivalent about permissiveness and coercion, evidencing their own confusion about how to act as parents, and how to live as adults in a stressful society. I would like to believe that much of our adolescent behavior is a healthy rebellion against the prejudices, the unhealthy attitudes and the hypocrisy of our generation of adults.

CHARLES P. GERSHENSON *Rarely does one person accumulate the varied experience of Charles Gershenson. Beginning as a research psychologist in the U.S. Air Force, he was next a teacher and experimentalist in social service research at Teachers College in New York City, and director of research of the Jewish Children's Bureau in Chicago. Thus prepared for work on a national scale, he became associate director of the research division of the U.S. Children's Bureau, and held that post for twelve years until it was given the coup de grace. During that time he was influential in helping establish important research programs in the care and education of very young children throughout the country.*

Combining this background and his later experience as a professor at Brandeis University and a consultant to UNICEF, he has become particularly knowledgeable about the making of public policy and is able to make valid comparisons between public planning for children's services in this country and similar programs in others. Gershenson has an unusually wide perspective and critical insight into a number of developments within his profession and within the whole range of services for children.

We've succeeded as a mental-health movement in convincing parents to look to the experts. Whether it's good for the mental health of the parents is another question.

MYRTLE MCGRAW *As the friend and colleague of some of the most renowned figures in the study of child development, particularly John B. Watson and Lawrence K. Frank, and a number of others tangentially related to that field, including John Dewey, Margaret Mead, and Frederick Tilney, Myrtle McGraw spent her entire professional life studying the behavior of infants. She is renowned for her naturalistic observations of the twins Johnny and Jimmy. She has always been innovative in the design and use of technical equipment to make her studies more objective.*

Similarly, she has been in the forefront in the experimental use of films for teaching undergraduate college students about infant care, believing that preparation for parenthood is best begun well before pregnancy occurs. One of her publications, Neuromuscular Maturation of the Human Infant, *is considered a classic.*

When I went to the Institute of Child Development at Teachers College in 1925, in connection with one of the courses I was supposed to do a study, a home study, of an infant. I'll never forget how funny it was because, if you'll remember, in those days behaviorism rigidities of management were in vogue and, together with a pediatrician's antiseptic attitudes, thumb-sucking was very bad. So when I walked into the baby's bedroom there at the home which I had selected to visit the first thing I saw was these braces on the thumb, and those lip tongue depressors on the elbow so that the baby couldn't get her thumb in her mouth, and she was blissfully sucking away on her great toe. John Watson had us put infants on the toilet every hour, almost on the hour, and you feed them at two o'clock, six o'clock, and weren't to take them up when they were crying, etc.

I think myself that if we could do more systematic studies of the process of growth in the first three years we would completely revolutionize our methods of child-rearing. All of these principles of learning that are in the textbooks and so forth are just not justifiable guidelines for bringing up a child during the first three or four years because they've been based on experimental procedures and others that focus on end results. My trademark is, "Let babies be the teachers."

This thing I would like to get across. There's nothing more exciting than the unfolding of behavior during the first three years. When you think of this little bit of protoplasm, right out of the uterus, and in three years he has to become human. He has to get on his two feet; he has to learn to talk, and in your language; and he can give you a damn good argument by three years. That's a fantastic development! Now, if you see it as something significant in what's happening in the process, nobody would ever have to tell you, "Be patient." Nobody would ever have to say, "Love them." We give these mothers guilt. "Do I love him or not? I'm supposed to. They tell me I've got to love him." Just stop to watch what the child is doing and patience is there—because you're interested.

I'm confident that we can recapture that—cultivate it in the preteeners and recapture it in the old ones. I was out to dinner with some people. . . . The daughter had worked with me with her baby and she had picked all this up by watching. Well, the baby was sitting at the table in a high chair and she dropped something down by the side. That grandmother, everyone, would have jumped a few weeks before to get it back to her. All of them stopped to see if she would recover it, and the father, who is a businessman, held his fork halfway between his plate and his mouth. I'm telling you this because it's enough to make me feel that we could begin to alter our cultural thinking and really influence the behavior even of, I think, a productive generation of parents. It's going to be harder unless they are actually involved because they are so harassed with such a multitude of things to do. In the home the telephone is ringing; they're collecting for this, they're . . .

Nobody gives a mother credit for what she does well. For years we've done nothing but blame them. We've got to add status and respect for the job of taking care of the young and provide excitement for those who do it. And I'm convinced it can be done, but I don't know how long it's going to take.

WILLIAM KESSEN

It's a little hard for me to be balanced about Watson. I guess it's very hard for anybody to be balanced about Watson. He was clearly a meteor or comet in the field. On the basis of his professional writings he comes through as one of the most unattractive human beings I can imagine. He may have been a jewel, and a kind of gentleman; in fact, his impact on the field has been almost completely deleterious. His attitude toward children, his attitude toward parents in *Psychological Care of Infant and Child* is, it seems to me, pathological. His impact on the Children's Bureau, and the child-care pamphlets that came out under the aegis of his students, was a most unfortunate development which took all of the force of your work and Spock's, too, to undo. If we turn from those aspects to some of his contributions to theory one can be more positive. As far as he touched the raising of children in America, I think it was totally a disaster.

I think that to blame the "permissive" era for whatever breakdowns in society there have been is not only a primitive formulation but wrong in a number of ways. If by "permissive" it is meant that we have been too easy on our children, I think that is false. I think we have put and continue to put undue demands for achievement and social flexibility on children. They have as adults gotten solutions that are inappropriate and primitive to major problems—faking being one of the most interesting ones and anxiety being one of the most hurtful. What I think the chatter about permissiveness does represent is a general diminution of conviction. It's not so much that we have failed our children in being too nice to them or giving them too many things; we have failed our children in not representing strong positions of our own. There's a kind of doubt about one's ideas, a doubt about one's beliefs, a kind of "I don't have an opinion on anything, you go solve the problem."

The shift outward, the shift away from the person to institutions not only for technical services, not only for technical administration and educational services, but for the resignation to those institutions of philosophical and ethical responsibility is a fact of the last fifty years in American culture. Those institutions either are not appropriate, cannot pick those functions up, or pick them up in a way that is so conflictive that the child is again left with no clear dimensions. But you can find hundreds of thousands of families in the United States, millions hopefully, in which the clear statement of what constitutes being an adult, what constitutes being a moral adult, what constitutes being a dutiful and contributing adult exists. And those children do not have the flaws, it seems to me, that they've been knocked for. So, it's not permissiveness of child-rearing that may have gotten us into a declining state, but the absence of strong moral imperatives.

J. MCVICKER HUNT   *This pioneer in child-development research is well prepared to assess the history of the movement, and because of his close personal relationships with most of the leaders in the field he is in a position to judge them and their work. His own recent research on cognitive learning and the role of experience, especially in the lives of children of preschool age and poor children, has made him an influential advisor to planners seeking to formulate educational programs for young children, whether in regional day-care centers or others under the aegis of the federal government.*

Hunt is professor emeritus of psychology at the University of Illinois. Of his many influential writings, among the most noteworthy is Intelligence and Experience.

John E. Anderson, who was director of the Institute of Child Welfare at the University of Minnesota through the late twenties and through the thirties and early forties and Arnold Gesell, who was director of the Yale Clinic for Child Development from 1911 to 1948, were in many ways opposite from John Watson in their interpretation of what was important in early development. Gesell, especially, emphasized the intrinsic growth within each individual that came from, presumably, genetic constitution. He minimized the role of experience in development and urged that parents allow their children a great deal of freedom and urged them to avoid pushing them at all costs.

John Anderson was perhaps more directly influential in an applied sense than Gesell. He pointed out that this attitude toward child-rearing was especially important in overcoming the one which had derived from the religious schools. I suppose I should mention here that schools for reading came out of the Reformation, when Luther and Calvin saw learning to read as a direct avenue to the word of God and salvation. When seven-year-old children found the Bible hard going, they saw this as evidence of original sin and Calvin was quite explicit in the notion that the child should be punished until he chose to learn. In fact, "Spare the rod and spoil the child" came out of Calvin's teaching, and one can say that he advocated beating the devil out of the child. Through most of the nineteenth century, laziness, slowness, lack of attentiveness were all evidences of sin, and the notion of a biologically determined rate of development, which could not be modified, took away the personal blame for being slow, or being inattentive, or not understanding, and

John Anderson was particularly anxious to get this change of view across to parents. How well he did it I can't say.

LOIS BARCLAY MURPHY *Lois Murphy has spent most of her professional life studying and teaching about children's development. Her research studies were made at Sarah Lawrence College, Menninger Foundation, and Bank Street College. At times she has collaborated with her husband Gardner Murphy, notably in their pioneer* Experimental Social Psychology, *and in their books on Western and Asian psychology.*

With a group of colleagues at the Menninger Foundation, Lois Murphy pursued studies of children through successive phases of physical, mental, and personality development. Theirs is one of the few longitudinal studies of child development from infancy through adolescence to receive a final synthesis. Books and articles growing out of this work document and discuss children's coping strategies and styles. The Widening World of Childhood, Paths Toward Mastery, Vulnerability, Coping, and Growth, *and* Adolescent Coping *are major volumes by Murphy's team.*

Infant and Child in the Culture of Today by Arnold Gesell and Frances L. Ilg and that whole series of books became a bible to many, many mothers before Spock came on the scene. And I've run into many mothers, from the time I began teaching at Sarah Lawrence in the thirties and on up, who said, "You know, Gesell has helped me so much; my child is doing exactly what he describes." And he, or Louis Ames, or one of the people around him, was very skillful in picking up quotations from their interviews with the mothers and observations of the children—such little things and yet so typical, typical still today. Say, the five-year-old's delight and excitement in saying, "I'm five!" And this kind of thing was very helpful in orienting mothers as to what to expect, so that in their descriptions of some of the troublesome things that come along at each age, the mothers' anxieties were relieved by knowing that this was to be expected. And Gesell was helpful also in this concept which, I think is much too over-simplified and yet basically has a soundness to it, of the alternation of periods of equilibrium and disequilibrium. The thing I object to about it is that he tends to date these at overly-precise periods—every six months or a year and so forth. But I still think mothers were very much helped just by knowing that you could expect this.

When I ran into mothers in supermarkets, for instance, I'd ask how the baby was. "Oh, he's fine; he's ahead of the Gesell norms on this and this and this, but I'm a little bit bothered he's behind on this." In other words they would take it too literally and too rigidly sometimes. Gesell did not have (I mean again from my point of view) enough awareness of the range of individual differences in the developmental picture. But I think he did an important thing for that time.

JOSEPH REID

As executive director of the prestigious Child Welfare League, Joseph Reid has been able to use his training and experience in social work as a critic, goad, and support for others working in institutions for children, as well as for those outside his profession who are (or should be) responsible for the welfare of children, especially those lacking satisfactory family and other nurturant care. His principles and standards of care are high, as they should be for those who are the advocates of children's rights.

In the last thirty years there has been one fashion, or fad, after another in the care of children. When I entered this field in the mid-thirties, for example, it was very, very easy to point to a significant fraction of children in residential treatment centers who were there at least in part because of the influence of an avant-garde publication of the U. S. Children's Bureau advising parents to be extremely permissive with their children; and those parents who could not handle permissiveness, particularly in the sexual area, did a lot of damage to kids when it was also combined with their own disabilities. Whenever someone seeks to build a whole system on Freudian psychology or behavior modification, etc., particularly a service-delivery system, I think we are in real danger. I can recall we have on several occasions brought Anna Freud to our conferences. One of her concerns, which was very well grounded, was that she hated ever to speak of a new theory addressed to a practical problem of care of children because it would be immediately picked up and applied as settled knowledge by practitioners who were extremely eager to do the right thing—overeager—and who were guided sometimes too much by those people who were considered to be the real leaders in the field.

BENJAMIN SPOCK

It was Reverend Norman Vincent Peale, Jr., who first accused me of corrupting a whole generation. He jumped on me one or two months after I was indicted by the federal government in January 1968. Peale said in his sermon here in New York that the reason there were so many irresponsible, undisciplined young people (by which he meant the ones who opposed the war in Vietnam, since he was a strong supporter of the war) was because I told their parents to give them "instant gratification" when they were babies. Those words "instant gratification" showed that Peale never looked at *Baby and Child Care*. . . . I got bushels of clippings of editorials and columns from newspapers all over the United States which picked up Peale's remark and said, "Of course, it's Spock who's raised this whole generation."

And Spiro Agnew made it practically a major campaign issue in the 1970 congressional elections. As I travel around the country I'm often asked by young people in university audiences with a very friendly smile, "How does it feel to be credited with a whole generation?" My feeling is, of course, that I would be tremendously proud if I thought that I played any large part, or even small part, in creating this idealistic and realistic generation. I do think that there is a slight connection and I figure it this way—that one of the sharpest differences between this generation of youths in the sixties and early seventies and earlier generations is that they can't be intimidated. They have an extraordinary independence of judgment.

Now, I think myself, that this is the influence primarily of Freud and of John Dewey, but as interpreted to parents by people like myself, which has made parents (especially college-educated liberal parents) have much more trust in their children. After all, Freud taught, in effect, that it's not discipline; it's love that makes good character. And Dewey said, "You don't have to cram knowledge down the throats of children; children are wild to learn if you give them appropriate material." I think that I popularized the basic ideas of Freud and Dewey in *Baby and Child Care* and said, "Your children are trying to grow up; they want to be more mature. Of course, you have to give them constant guidance because they're so inexperienced and so impulsive but they do the major part of the work." I think that that has been believed enough, especially by college-educated parents, that they've trusted their children's good intentions and have not set to work to intimidate them the way I was intimidated and the way children in general were intimidated by their parents in earlier generations.

Of course, there's another factor that has to be brought in, how so many conscientious parents have been rather scared of their children and afraid to discipline them, afraid to be too definite in their leadership, for fear that they'll distort their personalities or make their children hate them or at least not love them as much as they want to be loved. I think this is a fascinating and somewhat mysterious phenomenon: the parents of America being so nervous about doing right by their children. I suppose it has to do with the fact that we've been a country without traditions. And there is the mobility between the gen-

WHO TURN TO THE EXPERTS

erations so that young American parents have had to bring up their children relying on their own philosophy without being able to turn to the grandparents. So professional people in the children's sphere have acquired great authority in America that has made conscientious American parents constantly turn to them: "Don't just tell us what to do—but scold us and spank us for not having done right." And most of the American professional people couldn't resist the invitation to be didactic and scolding. To me it was a fascinating thing to find out years ago that it was Americans who read Freud and talked about Freud, that it wasn't Germans, French, and Austrians; those people went on the assumption that they knew how to raise children.

In my psychoanalytic training I was fascinated, of course, with all kinds of things. But I didn't learn anything that was directly applicable in pediatric practice. . . . After I'd been in practice five years, somebody came from Doubleday & Company to ask whether I would write a book on children. They came to me because they'd inquired of Leona Baumgartner or somebody, "Where is a pediatrician who also has some psychological training?" I said, with fright: "Oh, I don't know enough." And that wasn't because I was modest or even falsely modest. It's that I had not found the answers. . . . I was presumably in a position to give superior advice to parents because I'd had this psychological training, but it didn't give me any answers at all about breast-feeding or weaning or toilet-training, etc.

It wasn't until I'd been in practice for ten years (1943) when somebody came from Pocket Books and said, "Would you write a book on care of children?" This editor said with a leer, "It doesn't have to be very good. At 25 cents a copy we're going to be able to sell it in hundreds of thousands." I think it's very fortunate he said that because if he'd said, "We want this to be the best damn book that's ever been written," I would have worried a great deal whether I was capable of writing such a book and it would have taken me not three years but six or nine years to come up with it. But when he said, "I don't care whether it's very good," that sort of gave me permission to do the best I could and then be satisfied with it. So after ten years I really felt that I had learned enough from actual experience so that I had some perspective on psychoanalytic concepts.

When I was writing *Baby and Child Care* there were several things that were important to me: one was that it would be cheap so anybody could get it. It was 25 cents a copy when it first came out. It was unusually complete, being some 550 pages in the first edition, and, of course, it made a serious attempt to cope with not only physical health but psychological health, too. But I did have the idea right from the beginning of not scolding parents. I was perfectly well aware at the time that I wrote it that the stock in trade of most writers of books for parents was the scolding tone—taking the general attitude toward the reader, "Look out, stupid, you'll kill the child if you don't do exactly what I say." Hundreds and hundreds of times parents have said to me, "I remember that first sentence, 'You know more than you think you do. Don't be overawed by the expert'." And one of the things that has been most gratifying about the book, aside from the fact that I make my living from it and have been able to retire on it, is the fact that parents have responded to my confidence in them and my kindliness toward them.

I get relatively little straight fan mail. The overwhelming majority of the letters I get are problem letters. It's interesting to me that those problem letters always come in the same form. They always say, "Dear Dr. Spock: Your book has been generally helpful to me. However (they always use the word 'however') I have a problem that you haven't solved for me." (They usually refer to something that's very well covered in *Baby and Child Care*). Then, interestingly enough, having mentioned the problem, they go back and tell me all the good things about the child—it's a l-o-n-g paragraph. It says, "She has pink cheeks; she eats her spinach; she is agreeable and easy to manage most of the time." It's the third paragraph that says, "Well, now, about the real problem."

I think that my main achievement in helping parents to bring up their children was achieved not by telling them at what age they should get this or that inoculation or what age a child should begin to walk, but by giving them confidence in themselves. They say in letters, "It sounds as if you are talking to me and as if you think I'm a sensible person."

I'm still trying to give parents the self-confidence to lead their children. I've been writing magazine articles once a month for over twenty years now and I keep coming back to, "Don't be afraid of your child; you've got to lead her. If you do give her the leadership that she needs she'll not only be better behaved but she will be a happier child." This I believe absolutely. But it's only compulsiveness that makes me keep on repeating this because I don't see that lack of self-assurance in parents has diminished. I think the favor of it has changed now that young people are somewhat different but I think that parents are still afraid in one way or another of being as clear-cut as I think is ideal in child-rearing.

JUDITH SCHOELLKOPF *Trained at a time when Gesellian maturational theories were of great significance in child development, and later as a psychologist and a teacher of preschool children in the so-called Spockian era of permissiveness, Judith Schoellkopf has been able to observe the behavior of children and the response of parents to the different philosophies of child care espoused by the "experts." Although a Freudian by inclination and postgraduate training, she understands the dangers of oversimplification in the use of principles of that and any other ideology.*

At Harvard at this particular epoch, all of the fifties, young intellectual parents (the population was predominantly academic) were at that time right in the middle of being so permissive that their children, on the whole, were just dying to have some control. I used to really upset and startle students, parents, and visitors. They would hear the director walking into the room and say, "Cut it out." Kids were so delighted whenever they saw me, not because I always said, "Cut it out," but they knew that I would put my foot in if things were getting out of hand.

Certainly we know all about the extremely rigid upbringing era and how people started to try and break it up. Ben Spock was one of the biggest to be misinterpreted. On the part of those parents who were perhaps brought up very rigidly themselves, this was part of the whole atmosphere—"Boy, I'm not going to do to my child what was done to me." And, I think also that they became terrified of their children, terrified that it was like being square—if you told your child, "Now look, that's enough" —it was like being square today. Therefore, they got on the bandwagon to just let these kids run. I don't think it is true that Freudian theory stimulated permissiveness. I think that is a misunderstanding of Freud, a misinterpretation, and I think that Anna Freud would agree with me completely.

LOIS MEEK STOLZ *No one in the child development movement has had a more distinguished and varied career than Lois Stolz. To achieve her position, she had to overcome many obstacles, since in this field, as in others, women have rarely been given the opportunity for work or the compensation they deserve. She was a pioneer in establishing day-care centers for children of working mothers, a promoter of the education of women, a writer-teacher on the subject of child-rearing, especially the rearing of preschoolers, and a founder of organizations concentrating on research in child development. As an administrator, she promoted research and directed varied programs for education and training. She is professor emerita of psychology at Stanford University.*

I think that we're very likely, whenever we're having any kind of difficulty, to say that this is because of the way children were raised. *First,* we said that the difficulty was that they were all raised too strictly according to the Watsonian plan of conditioning, and without enough affection and love. *And now,* we say that we have hippies because the parents raised them too permissively. My own feeling is that both of these phenomena stem from the culture rather than from the child-rearing practice. Now, this doesn't mean that there aren't some children who do not have enough structure, that many families have not found the way of giving structure and freedom, because both are important in a child's life. But it also means that there are many parents that have found the way to do this, and that there are many people raised today who are much more creative than they would have been if they had been raised on the old, strict, authoritarian kind of pattern. An authoritarian kind of pattern of strict obedience and punishment does not build creative people, and it's only by accident that we get them.

Personally, I don't like the word *permissive*. I like the word *lenient* . . . meaning that such a person builds his child-rearing practices on the basis of the needs of his child whatever age he is, at whatever stage of development, because children have different needs at different times.

ORVILLE G. BRIM, JR. *Brim is one of two prominent sociologists (John Clausen is the other) with a long record of interest in child development. As the president of the Foundation for Child Development in New York City, he is in a position to foster research and innovative service programs that cannot attract governmental funding. Brim has spent a large portion of his career "trying to get more social science into public policy information." His* Education for Child Rearing *is considered a classic.*

When I wrote that book on parent education, *Education for Child Rearing,* and summarized all the literature for parents up to 1955 . . . there's no more than a few pages, I think I said, in the literature for parents of the past three decades dealing with cognitive development. It's all social-emotional development. You'd think the child had no brain and was not concerned about learning anything except affectivity. And in the 1970s you could look back on the research and literature for parents during the past twelve years, and the social-emotional materials have virtually disappeared. It's all cognition—books for parents on how to develop your child's IQ, on early infant stimulation. The toys are all cognitive development toys and stimulators, rather than fuzzy animals and other things that are supposed to develop affect. It's dramatic.

JEROME KAGAN *Like many other researchers in child development, Kagan came into the field "by accident," having originally planned a career in the physical sciences. One of the leaders in the field, Kagan's research in perceptual and attentive functioning in infants and in their cognitive processes received wide attention and publicity and accounted, in the 1970s, for much of the stress placed on the critical importance of early stimulation for learning in later life. As a consequence, mothers were made to feel another vital responsibility for determining children's success or failure academically and intellectually.*

As Kagan expanded his research, he softened his earlier verdict and concluded that children are "more resilient than any of us surmise," and that he "could not hold onto the notion that there are some irreversible consequences because of infancy." He is professor of developmental psychology in the Faculty of Arts and Sciences and a member of the Faculty in Education, Harvard University. Of his numerous publications, perhaps the most provocative is "Cross Cultural Perspectives on Early Development" in the November 1973 American Psychologist.

I'm not sure all the influence of child psychologists on childrearing has been all good. For example, when child psychology shifted from being concerned with the quality of the interpersonal relationship between caretaker and child, under psychoanalytic influence, to a concern with intellectual variables, then, as you know, mothers became more concerned with whether their children would be smart than whether they'd be free of anxiety and secure.

DAVID ELKIND   *Although an academician, Elkind does not place narrow limits on his interests. He reaches beyond his field of developmental psychology to teach those in other fields as an interpreter of such masters as Freud and Piaget. He is well aware of the difficulties of American families in child-rearing and is sympathetic toward all those who struggle with the inherent problems such responsibility involves. Elkind is professor and director of graduate training in developmental psychology at the University of Rochester.* Child Development: A Core Approach *expresses his concepts of child development.*

I think that twenty years ago we were much more child-centered than we are today. I think child-centering is like permissiveness; I think it's probably dead. Twenty years ago you'd talk to parents and they were very much concerned about the emotional well-being of children. Today they're concerned about intellectual stimulation and growth, and parents today are increasingly, because of women's liberation and a variety of other things, not placing the child's needs ahead of their own and giving them priority. I think they're seeing that their needs have equal value with their child's and therefore are more willing to break up marriages and such. I don't think it's bad; I'm simply saying that there's a more egalitarian notion about child-rearing, that the child's intellectual and emotional independence is demanded much earlier.

I really believe that child development is used by the populists to fit their own needs and that often perhaps parents will find in the literature that which meets their needs at the time. There are going to be a variety of positions—breast-feeding, nonbreast-feeding—and what parents will pick up will be what fits in with their own point of view. It's a little bit like the early stimulation. It's my feeling that many mothers took this as a rationalization for their own wish to get out of the home. "I'm not providing my child with appropriate stimulation if I don't send him to nursery school." So they have a rationalization for not wanting to stay home with the kids, whereas before "I'm somehow not a woman if I don't do this" was their feeling. Now she has a good excuse for not doing so. "I'm not a good mother if I don't provide the stimulation." So often, I think, child-development literature can be used to fit in with the parent's own needs, and there's always a give and take. It's never one-sided.

LEE SALK

The parent has a problem, the kind of problem that I call a "normal" problem. . . . "How do I deal with my child's rebelliousness?" or "How do I deal with my child who all of a sudden decides he or she doesn't want to go to school today?" Generally, the parent turns to the pediatrician, and the pediatrician gives advice. Frankly speaking, having been in a pediatrics department for a long time, and having spent time in various universities, I can tell you that pediatricians are not trained to deal with these questions, and yet the pediatrician answers the question with authority, as if he or she knows the answer. Now, this is how I think a lot of misinformation has gotten through to parents. I think this is the way that many myths that are totally unscientific have been perpetuated. The only way a person could get mental-health support, or help, in the past, had been by having a problem that was so very substantial that psychiatric help was required, but for anything short of a psychiatric problem, you had to go to your pediatrician. And I always felt there was a big gap that ought to be filled by some mental-health professional, and this is what I call pediatric psychology.

What I am trying to do is to take the knowledge and information I have acquired in my training as a psychologist, distill it and transmit it to the consumer. To me, the consumer is the parent, the pediatrician, the nurse, the teacher, all the health professionals. Now, pediatricians do not read psychological journals, and psychologists do not generally publish in pediatric journals, so we run into a problem of transmitting, of cutting across the barrier—it's worse than the placental barrier—to get information from behavioral theory to the practitioner. This is why pediatricians still say, "Newborn babies can't see," in spite of the fact that research in psychological laboratories shows they do see, and that they can distinguish complicated visual objects from uncomplicated ones, and so on.

I am absolutely convinced that children who are brought up in an environment where their needs are not met, particularly during the first year of life, suffer a great deal—not just in terms of emotional pain, but they literally learn to tune out the world. It's a frustrating world for them; they have very few resources available to cope with that kind of stress and they are inclined to go off to sleep as a means of obliterating the unpleasantness. Children who are picked up and held a great deal want to be picked up and held, and they seek out much more stimulation; they turn to adults in an attempt to have their needs satisfied. There's a lot of data that's been gathered on these problems. And I know that some people will say, "Well, these are not terribly significant, or terribly good experiments." René Spitz demonstrated that babies who were not picked up sufficiently developed autistic-like symptoms and depression, anaclitic depression. . . . I have seen a number of children who have begun to show autistic-like features in their behavior after periods of crying it out, and this is generally done at the recommendation of a pediatrician who feels that crying is good for the lungs, that you have to teach your baby that you are not going to be there even if he or she wants you. Babies do stop crying eventually, if parents do not respond, but I think this is dangerous. They are helpless and passive and stop crying because they've given up hope of getting help. They withdraw into sleep as their only defense. So, I encourage the parents to respond to their babies' needs, particularly when they are passive and dependent.

Many people have blamed Dr. Spock for being too permissive. This is not true. Dr. Spock believed in setting limits. However, he is the one who has recommended that you let a baby cry it out. He believes in other things I would disagree with. I don't believe in giving people recipes for child-rearing. In my own writings, I have made an attempt to provide parents with the knowledge I think they need to have to solve their *own* problems, rather than use a cookbook approach—or recipes—on what to do, or what not to do. In other words, I could say, "You should always pick up your baby when it cries" (I must say, I *have* said that on a number of occasions) but I much prefer to explain to parents what happens if you pick up your baby and what happens if you don't pick up your baby, and let them decide.

You see, it's not only philosophically that I differ with Spock, but I think there's a difference in emphasis. Spock emphasized the physical care of the child, but did give parents a great deal of reassurance that they didn't have to worry about those specific stages of development. I think that his predecessors, the Gesells, were inclined to map out the development of children, and parents were turning to Gesell before the Spock book came out. They were checking if the child was doing the right thing at the right time, and many parents were very anxious about that. Spock came along and said, "Don't worry about those things; children are different individuals." And I certainly agree with him on that. He took away the anxiety parents had and I think that made a major change in terms of child-rearing practices.

I think Spock has been misunderstood, and I think maybe he has not clarified certain points that I feel have been crucially important. While I believe in indulging babies and meeting their needs, I don't mean that you *continue* to indulge the child forever. As a child begins to show greater independence, as the child begins to do things with his or her hands and crawls from one place to another, you have to begin to set limits. The general approach has been to be completely permissive with a child throughout its life, or to start out with rules and regulations

WHO TURN TO THE EXPERTS

before the child has an understanding of rules and regulations; I think neither one provides the optimal environment for growth and development. I think you have to respond to the child's developing needs and help the child learn to cope with his or her own resources in order to be able to deal with life's problems. I believe an effective parent is the one who teaches the child to utilize his or her own resources at each stage in development. That requires development of trust in the parent during the first year. If you do not establish that trust in the first year, I think the communication process can break down between the child and the parents.

Many people who have set up programs in parent education are not teaching parenthood; they are teaching child development and there is a distinct difference. Anyone can learn the milestones of development . . . but it is very difficult to get across the concepts of the nitty-gritty problems of the everyday activities of a parent. For example, waking up, not being able to have a hot cup of coffee in the morning for many weeks on end because of the responsibilities. . . . I am urging more people to consider not having any children at all, without feeling a stigma attached to this decision. I think that there is nothing wrong with a person making a positive choice not to have children. I think we have to get across the idea that parenthood is one of the most important roles a human being can take on in life. We, as professionals, have to elevate the role of parenthood to the point where people pay more respect to those who take on that role. I think that rearing a child is a very time-consuming occupation; it takes a lot of energy and some people are just temperamentally not suited for it. That's why we have child abusers. Had these people known of the patience required to handle a child they might have said, "This is not for me," and they should be free to select this.

When I was doing my internship at the University of Michigan I rotated through a well-baby clinic at the University Hospital and I was impressed by the number of questions those parents—mostly mothers—had. They were *anxious* in dealing with their children and I realize now that that anxiety was normal anxiety . . . which a pediatrician is often inclined to interpret as an "overanxious" mother, or an "overprotective" mother. The species never would have survived had they not had that normal, natural protective feeling. Calling a mother an anxious mother only makes her defensive and, perhaps, hostile, and it undermines her confidence. This makes parents feel as if parenthood is not important. It also makes them feel that by following their natural inclinations they are probably bound to do all the wrong things.

I found that these parents were asking rather simple questions and they were getting rather stupid answers. I must admit that I was singularly impressed by the stupidity of the answers given by doctors, by nurses, by health professionals, and they were also somewhat condescending. And this, of course, is one reason why parents read anything they can get their hands on. They are seeking help. They are vulnerable to any kind of information because basically they want to do what is best for the child. I have never seen a parent—unless the person is really seriously emotionally disturbed—whose interest is not doing the best for the child. They want to follow professional advice, but unfortunately many of the professionals have given the wrong advice. In this way I think we have failed. Parents will follow advice but we have given them the wrong advice: "Let a baby cry, it's good for their lungs!" This is nonsense!

Some twenty-odd years later, I am just as impressed by the simplicity of the questions and the stupid answers they are getting from health professionals. And this is what led me to direct my interest to parent education on all fronts. While I am an advocate of parent education, I think a great deal of damage can be done through parent education. I would say that the majority of books for parents are not written by professionals; they are written by self-styled experts who are more like journalists who have gone around interviewing people like you and me, and then feel that once they have picked our brains they can sit down and write a book of their own. And parents will accept some of these. I think that the need for "recipes" on child-rearing has led many people to pick up books that will say, "If you want to toilet train your child in no time, all you do is to give your child a reward, or pennies, or gold stars or something like that." This does not help a child understand the process of self-mastery that is necessary in toilet training.

I think that child-rearing advice over the years has been like a swinging pendulum—maybe not completely, but there was a period of time when the behaviorists believed in reinforcement and now we are back to behavior modification. And I am a little unhappy with that, because I find these behavior-modification people saying things like, "If you pick up your baby when it cries and satisfy it, you are reinforcing crying." I think it's incorrect. It's as incorrect as saying that when you are hungry and you sit down at the dinner table and eat your dinner you are reinforcing hunger. I recall the behaviorists in the thirties and early forties who said, "Pinch the baby to make it cry because crying provides exercise." So parents followed that advice.

Even some of the current child-development literature is incorrect. I've seen statements like "Babies don't smile until they are two or three months of age." This is absolute nonsense. We've all seen babies smile in their first two or three days of life. It usually occurs at the end of a feeding when the baby retracts the facial muscles, which I believe is for the purpose of detaching itself from the mother, and then goes off to sleep. They call that "gas." I've heard doctors and nurses say this. When parents ask me about this I generally ask them: "Have you ever really thought this through? Have you ever had gas? I've had gas and it doesn't make me smile. Why should a baby smile when it has gas?" Perhaps here is where my psychological training comes in handy. I'll say, "Let's look at that statement; how did it develop?" Probably some astute observer once heard a baby pass gas while it smiled, at the end of a feeding, and said, "Aha, the baby is not smiling; it's gas." Well, the reverse could have been true—smiling causes gas. Obviously this is absurd. It's the kind of questioning approach that I am trying to get across.

Take the notion that babies can't see when they are first

born. Babies look their mothers right straight in the face during their early feedings. Sometimes it's the first feeding, or second feeding. When I point this out, the mothers generally smile and say, "It makes me think that maybe my baby knows that I am its mother." They feel marvelous until some doctor or nurse comes along and says, "No, your baby can't see, and it won't be able to see until it's two, or three, or four, or five, or eight weeks of age." So, the mother, of course, is discouraged. And I say to these mothers: "Why would the baby look you straight in the face if it couldn't see you?" She'll say, "Well, my doctor says that maybe the baby can see, but it can only see shapes and shadows." And I say, "Well, what am I? Look at me. What do you see if you had to describe your actual retinal experience?" "Why, you are shapes and shadows." "Well, that's right. What the doctors are doing, in effect, is demeaning you as a parent; they are saying: 'You are not important, your baby can't even see you, you're only a shape or a shadow, he can't even relate to you. You are neurotic because you want to make him happy and pick him up; and besides, you can interfere with his physical health by interfering with his lung structure because crying is good for the lungs!'"

BOYD MCCANDLESS *This eminent psychologist was interviewed because he had a great deal of experience in the field of child development and because he has a special interest in parent education. His concern extended to parents ranging from prosperous Iowa farmers to the poor blacks of the South. He viewed Head Start as an important vehicle for education of preschool children of parents in all social classes. At the time of his death in 1975 he was professor and director of educational psychology at Emory University in Atlanta.*

I have no hope for parent education being effectively carried out with any of the old styles. I think possibly a new look in day care (and I'm intensely interested in day care these days), with more emphasis on sensitivity training, the types of interaction, the change of attitudes, rather than the old preachments, may indeed succeed. I think parent education is fundamental; I do think parents can be changed. My involvement with the parent-child center with poor black mothers here in Atlanta does suggest to me that certainly many of them are changed, but by *their* definition. They do become better parents as an aspect of a new look in parent education, some of which comes from psychiatry, some from education, some from dynamics and sociology, some from economics.

I think that the exploration of your own feelings about race, hostility, dependency (of course, in the South we're particularly sensitive to race and may be coming along, you know, remarkably well in solving it, at least in a place like Atlanta), your own power needs, the conflict between power needs and the needs of children . . . have to be worked out in staff training for places like day-care centers and in parent education. And parents have to come face to face with what they think about rebellion, about autonomy, about dependency, about emergent sexuality, about adolescence, and all manner of things. And as they begin to understand themselves then will their parent-child relations improve.

SHELDON WHITE

I believe that what really happens in education and in child day care depends very deeply on the minds of 2 million teachers and 50 million parents and the way they see children and the way they deal with children. I think if you can change their minds, if you can make them see human nature more completely, that they respond better to children. . . . No book ever written about child-rearing means a goddamn thing—it's what's in the mind of the mother. No book for teachers about learning theory means anything—it's what's in the mind of the teacher.

3 After Millions Spent on Research, What Do We Know about Children?

We know nothing of childhood; and with our mistaken notions the further we advance the further we go astray.

Rousseau, Émile, *1780*

Lawrence Frank told me that when he persuaded the Laura Spelman Rockefeller Memorial to launch a large-scale program for the study of children in 1923–24, "the general theory was . . . that we knew little or nothing about children." In the years since then immense efforts and a great deal of money—it is impossible to calculate just how much—have been expended to fill that knowledge gap. Research studies have been carried on at Harvard, Yale, the University of California, the University of Iowa, the University of Minnesota, Western Reserve, the University of Colorado, the University of Michigan, Syracuse, Antioch, Cornell, Columbia, Vassar, Sarah Lawrence, the Mayo Clinic, Stanford, the University of Rochester, and these are only some of the places which have been or still are involved in such work. In addition, individuals have pursued their studies supported by research grants, and, since World War II, the federal government has become involved to a very substantial degree, either by providing grants to outside institutions and individuals or by carrying on work within its own agencies. An indication of the size of federal involvement is given in the 1974 annual report of the Interagency Panel on Early Childhood Research and Development, which reviewed federal research activities during that year. This report, which dealt only with the early childhood field, described 2,307 projects administered by seventeen federal agencies with a total budget of $239.1 million. It further explained that another 310 projects funded for over $59 million had been left out because of lack of information at the time the report went to press.

At first the research institutes concentrated largely on observations and measurements of normal children. In a brief historical review of the study of children, Marian Radke-Yarrow and Leon J. Yarrow observed, "Data were carefully collected on every aspect of child development and behavior which was amenable to a behavioristic approach of objective measurement and testing. Sex and age differences were the primary points of comparison. Heredity as opposed to environment, and maturation as opposed to training constituted organizing frameworks for many research projects. Except for this theoretical controversy, child psychology was essentially atheoretical."

After a period when child psychology "stood still," the Yarrows said: "Childhood re-emerged as a crucial field of study . . . when testable hypotheses based on clinical (mainly psychoanalytic) theories began to be formulated by systematically oriented researchers, when psychological theory and cultural anthropology converged and when the genius of Kurt Lewin [a Gestalt psychologist] trained the experimental method upon meaningful social psychological questions within a framework of dynamic field theory." *

With the enthusiasm for the cognitive theories of Jean Piaget, which accelerated after the successful launching of Sputnik into orbit in 1957 had convinced Americans that something had to be done about education in this country, research began to center on the learning processes. The enormous concentration on cognitive development in the early years of life that followed continued into the early 1970s. Now, however, the spotlight is shifting to other aspects of development. The annual report of the Interagency Panel on Early Childhood Research and Development of 1972 is an indicator of this trend. In discussing the research plans of the federal agencies, it commented: "Holistically-oriented research, including research related to the 'total child' and to the child's 'total life space' has increased both in the FY '73 planning and FY '74–'78 planning. Also, more of the agencies represented are planning to increase research in social-emotional and physical development, while giving less attention to the study of cognitive development as an element unrelated to other aspects of child growth. This reiterated the intent to study the child reacting as a total entity to the forces and influences in the environment."

The point is that in the last fifty years or so a huge collection of studies of children from all walks and conditions of life, inspired by ever-changing theoretical and practical considerations

* Yarrow and Yarrow, "Child Psychology," *Annual Review of Psychology* 6 (1955): 1–2.

and carried out with a wide assortment of research designs, has been accumulated. The question remains, however: "What does it all add up to?" I felt that it was of central importance to explore with my interviewees the actual progress that has been made in our "hard" knowledge since the days when Frank acted on the premise that "we knew little or nothing about children."

JEROME KAGAN

What do we know about children? Let me begin the answer (I don't mean to be pedantic) by agreeing with the philosopher Karl Popper, whom I admire. Scientific progress is usually marked by the elimination of bad ideas; it is a reduction in ignorance, because what we need to know is infinite. We have made progress in the last fifty years because we have, through thought and empirical work, eliminated some incorrect ideas. Babies don't have to be fed every four hours; you don't have to initiate toilet-training between year one and two. That's progress. But compared to modern biology we're a sixteenth-century science.

We now appreciate something that we didn't appreciate fifty years ago: not only is motor development under maturational control, which everyone had acknowledged, but we now know, thanks to the elegant work of Piaget, Kessen, Fantz, and others, that the perceptual, symbolic, and memory systems are also under maturational control, and the work on language has been important here. Well, that's an important insight—to recognize that experience does not completely control cognitive development.

We also suspect that the major changes in cognitive development have to do with new strategies, how one deals with information rather than the hardware of the nervous-system. It's not that the computer gets much better; it's that the *program* gets richer. That's a very important insight.

I think—and this is more controversial—that one must attend less to the material experiences of the child and more to the child's perception of experience—what is seen as change or variability from the child's point of view. That is to say, one cannot answer the question "What is the effect of punishment on a child?"—a question we used to ask thirty years ago. We must ask, "What is this child's prior expectation from his parents?" If he's normally punished, then failure to punish may affect him more than a punishment, if you're trying to change his behavior. If he's normally praised a punishment will be more effective. That is to say, the child has a "tote" board of expected outcomes, and what will alert his attention and recruit his motivation is an event he is not accustomed to. It's very important to acknowledge the relativism in the child's commerce with his environment. . . . Parents still ask at PTA meetings, "How many hours a week should a father be with his child?" "Is punishment good or bad?" I think we've learned those are inappropriate questions. That is an advance.

We know very little about the mother-infant relationship. We know that a child will become attached to more than one caretaker. John Bowlby led some people to believe that a child could attach himself only to one. I think we know that there's no specific set of practices a mother must initiate—a recipe for child rearing can't be written, but the important dimensions include consistency, regularity, and variety. . . . How many times a parent kisses a child or how and when one feeds are less important. It's not in the specific actions but in the melody those actions comprise—consistency, continuity, regularity, variety. Of course, that suggestion has to be proven; it is a hypothesis that some of us hold. But when one views development through these lenses, one asks different questions about development.

ELIZABETH WICKENDEN

I'm naturally interested in all aspects of social science and life but I am very fearful of the effort to dehumanize it, to put everything on a computer, to think every public function must show a cost-benefit or a direct cause-and-effect relationship. I think many things that influence human behavior, human well-being, human functioning are really beyond the scope of measurement and should perhaps remain so. They come into the area of poetry and art and general humanity.

SHELDON WHITE

I think we know a great deal about children in a general sort of estimated kind of sense. I would say that I am fascinated by the sequence that goes from Herbert Spencer to James Mark Baldwin to Werner to Piaget and the ethologists of today. I see that as basically a broad vision of human development. Wrong in particulars but basically getting refined, getting mapped more and more, data being reissued in each generation in another system, in another scheme. I believe that we do have—I don't know how to put it—more sophisticated intuitions about children. We don't know any more about children than, let's say, Rousseau did in the eighteenth century. There have always been —throughout history—men who had very gifted intuitions about children.

I'd say that what we learned about children in the practice of philosophy, biology, psychology has acted not to give us definite knowledge but to reduce uncertainty. We now believe —we are not sure—that there is a kind of sensitive period for the laying down of language up to age six or up to age twelve, but we believe that early in life vaguely something having to do with lateralization has something to do with the way in which language is established. We don't definitely know how to cure aphasia or anything else but we have restricted the uncertainties; we are sort of hunting in a closer area. We believe now that there is some kind of an important attachment process and that it's related to mother contact or caretaker contact and that the sensitive period, or the major period, is between six months and three years of age—possibly up to ten years of age, according to Bowlby. We believe that there is a growth of what has been called "mental athleticism" which peaks about eighteen and is over at twenty-five, and we believe that there is a crystallized intelligence which, sort of, goes up steadily with age. Now, all of those things are not very definite but yet they considerably reduce uncertainty. My guess is that a man who manages a government program, a man who designs a curriculum at the high school or the college level, because in the past they've exceeded those estimates, are now constrained within boundaries or led to do things that are more realistic about people. So, let's say that we are reducing the range of irrational variation.

DAVID ELKIND

It's really been one of our big problems that American social science has been so concerned with esoteric cultures, foreign places, and so on, that we really haven't studied very closely the cultures within our society. An anthropologist has to go to South America before a sociologist will focus on a particular aspect of society, the delinquents or something. The ethnic variation within our society, I guess perhaps because it's the myth of the melting pot that we are all alike and that therefore there's no sense in studying differences, we haven't really studied systematically. A lot of our problems, I think, in misinterpreting data are that we simply say it's genetic or experiential and we leave out the whole possible range of cultural differences within our society to account for individual differences. Some of the Jensen stuff, I think, fails for just this reason. He equated people's socioeconomic status, blacks and whites, and assumed therefore that the culture is the same. That is a very different culture, even though the socioeconomic status is the same. We have ruled out a whole realm of variables or variations. . . . We don't know enough to say very clearly about cultural groups.

In a general sense, I see three parameters of child development. First of all, the child is a knowing organism—he seeks out knowledge, seeks information, seeks out novel kinds of things. He's a showing organism—he seeks to express himself, to talk about, to demonstrate not only in language but in play and so on, what he knows; he wants to communicate. And he's a growing organism—he's constantly changing. Specifically, from my own research, clinical work and so on, I'm terribly impressed with the general stages that Piaget talks about in terms of cognitive development. Without tying them especially to particular ages and so on, I'm just very impressed with the significant changes that come about in children's thinking between four and six and between eleven and fifteen and the limitations that that kind of thinking imposes upon the ways in which children interact with their peers and the ways that they learn and so on. And in my own work I've been trying to spell out some of the implications of these limitations for working with children and for teaching parents child rearing—particularly in the areas of the interpersonal domain which Piaget has not expanded upon.

In addition, I think the point that is very difficult for people to get—and yet I think it is so central—is that the child from the very beginning is creating and constructing cognitive knowledge about the world and that he is never simply copying the external world nor is he simply reflecting ideas; so that his intellectual growth, his social growth is always not only just taking over from the inside or maturing, but it's a constant restructuring, rethinking, correcting errors; it's, if you will, a hypothesis testing, checking. It's never this empty vessel that we're just pouring into, or . . . a filled vessel but rather the child is constantly interacting and changing and the crucial point is that he's always creating, that even the material he takes from the outside is never simply imitated. This means that in parent-child interactions or teacher interactions the problems of communication and understanding are crucial. In talking with teachers and parents I again and again emphasize the importance of listening, of communication, and how difficult it is to understand a child and how difficult it is for a child to understand us. Before we can educate or rear we have to begin to try to understand. So these are the kinds of things that I argue as being crucial.

CHARLES P. GERSHENSON

Let me, from a broad viewpoint in terms of child development, say we've learned a tremendous amount on the physical side and have a tremendous body of knowledge about the genetic components of prenatal life, the fetal development, the delivery, the immediate period thereafter. We have the technology and the knowledge for the most part now to insure that most children are well-born. By well-born I mean a birth weight we'll say of 2501 grams or better, free of any congenital defects. When you get something like in Sweden where we're down to eight or nine per thousand dying in the first year you're reaching the level where science alone will hardly go below that. When we reached twenty we thought that would be it. So physically I think we've made tremendous strides. The knowledge is there. Is there a will now to do what needs to be done. That's a political issue and a social issue.

Okay, in psychology now in relation to the child itself. I think the experiences of the sixties which sort of put child psychology on the front burner—"Here are children, here are issues, the government will support you, what should we do?"—and then the cumulative finding that not everything worked as well as we wanted has shaken up the psychological profession. It's shaken up the profession between what they've been studying in the laboratory, what they've been studying with their beautifully done experiments, and the translation into large-scale national kinds of programs. And they don't see any more of the one-to-one relationships, which raises questions of the following: One, was my basic knowledge wrong? Two, if my knowledge was right, then was it simply a question of administrative failure? Or third, as some people have argued . . . we're drawing conclusions, negative ones particularly, too early. In other words, the data are not all in and we should wait.

I think though that the field has begun to reexamine—the

child-development field, the child-psychology field particularly—in terms of the nature of the problems it was studying, how it went about studying the issues and what can we say at this particular point are the universals and what are specific to our culture and our techniques. And the more ethnographic studies are coming to life, the more we're beginning to see how culturally bound we are within the nature of both the techniques and the studies. I think the whole questioning of IQ had a positive effect in that we had for so many years such great confidence in it and used it, you know, as an absolute scale in so much psychological testing. To begin to even question that and begin then not only questioning its limitations but examining why it was limited has now thrown us open to examining all our instruments, all our approaches. So that I think we're in a period of readjustment. We're not willing to talk at this particular point, until we integrate our thinking, as to what are the absolute knowns and in what direction we should move ahead.

About child development at the present time I think we're in full agreement of the greater importance than we believed before of the early period of life, the first six years (as a matter of fact, of the prenatal, the fetal period as well), particularly in terms of physiological development. But we're not accepting any more Bloom's thesis which reflects decades-ago thinking . . . that by age four 50 percent of the intellectual development of the child can be accounted for. It's not a statement that he himself has held to. It was a momentary kind of statement and I think that it's one of these distortions . . . that gets bandied about. So, by importance I mean the following. We're aware that the child learns a great deal more and is using all sense modalities in the learning process and that we are not yet able to fully perceive and understand all the learning that is going on within the child. Our instrumentation is not good; but it's internal, we know it's there and we see it in certain behavior manifestations on the part of the child occurring at an earlier age and in a more integrated fashion than we had thought before.

A mothering person appears to play a key role in this,

whether it's a biological or psychological mother. . . . It does appear (or it's my bias) that it's the continuity—the continuity, particularly in the initial couple of years, of a familiar mothering figure. That is the person who enables the child to perceive and understand the world and the sensitivity of that integration greatly affects both the nature of the learning, the interest in learning, and the development. And this not only affects, in effect, cognition but the emotional tone and relatedness. It affects the actual physical integration with the learning, the psychomotor, the sensory-motor, integration and development that occurs. A passive approach is not sufficient at all. In other words, there has to be an active participation with the child. The child is simply not an unfolding flower concept nor is it the other concept—simply a bundle of id impulses that one has to tame and control under any circumstances.

Another thing we've learned is the importance of language and so new thinking. . . . Definitely, the language development is one of the key issues. I think the work of Larry Kohlberg and others has given us a much firmer understanding of something which we neglected and dropped—the whole issue of the moral development of children which sort of faded away as we became excited about the cognitive development of children. And it's interesting, we're getting in so many areas now—whether you call them phases or stages, there is evidentially a hierarchical evolvement of moral development, a hierarchical development in terms of cognitive kind of development. It will not surprise me to see coming out similar thoughts about affective development. I think we're beginning to see this now in the areas of socialization as well. What we are lacking are the specifics.

WILLIAM KESSEN

Most of the things that we talk about as unassailable in our knowledge of child development are for I guess what is called the average expectable environment. That is, "in 85 percent of the cases the following will be true" is the way I think it has to be said. And the way I would prefer to say it is . . . "that within wide boundaries the following principles hold." The physical growth principles are I think the most defensible ones. There are certain clear behavioral maturational issues (as they used to be called, although I think that is a funny name for them), there are regularities in development, which are unassailable. The child will walk at roughly such a time, and he will talk at roughly such a time; he will be able to solve certain problems at such a time—not necessarily because he has a program to do so in the center of his head, but because there are *such* regularities in his development and *such* regularities in the environment to which he is exposed that these things are inevitably pulled along. And I think a fundamental misconception of Piaget is to cast him as a maturational theorist. What he's taught me, in part, is that there are such regularities in the environment that infants meet that they with their own biological predispositions are drawn to be the kind of child that one particularly sees at the end of one year or at the end of two. Not that he could not be different, but this joint regularity almost guarantees certain emergent patterns. I think that some of the changes that take place at adolescence also fall into this predictable and regular category.

Now, aside from those, which are really regularities of behaviors, it seems to me there are underlying regularities of strategy in kids. And that's why we come to this notion of adaptation. What we can see—and perhaps it's the only regularity across development—is that the child brings to any situation a system of expectation, a system of theories about how it works. And those theories will be modified or employed as a function of what kind of confirmation or disconfirmation he gets. We can roughly categorize those for middle-class children in the United States, and in a sense that is what Piaget and some of his American imitators have done. What we have been very, very hard pressed to do is to put the parameters on that—to have statements of the following sort: "Under the following range of environmental variation the following behaviors will emerge." All the conversation about nature and nurture, it seems to me, has been off that parametric point. We don't need to make yes/no decisions; we need to set up a whole set of probabilistic functions that say, "Within such and such an environmental variation you get such and such a pattern." So I guess that the regularities of development that I would like to defend are those which seem to be relatively insensitive to minor environmental change. And I think there really are such things.

The child has to be presented with the form of problems that he can handle. Implicit in much of the early writing on mother-infant interaction and explicitly in Piaget and in some of Kagan's recent observations, the notion of optimal lead, which is an old educational one, is fundamental. That is, the child cannot handle a problem that puts too great a demand on his present theoretical structure, except by making reduced diminished solutions. Much of the failure of the poor and the black in conventional school settings has to do with making minimal solutions because the problems which have been posed exceed the capacity of the child to deal with them. So he's made a solution, he's solved the problem that has been presented to him; it's just that the wrong problem has been presented or the wrong relation exists between the problem and what he can do. So that when you speak of continuity, I would speak either of predictability or problem-appropriate solutions. Now those two are related in a rather complicated way. Clearly a child who has continuing relation to a single other person, a single mother, is better able to make predictions about her behavior and her response to him; there's sort of an automatic way in which the problems are presented to him in a graded fashion because they both know what the system is like. And clearly the more new people that come into that process the more often it's going to be discombobulated either because the adult doesn't know what the kid is like or because he makes a prediction which is disconfirmed.

The boundary condition on that for full development to take place is that the child has to be continually presented with new problems. What we're looking for is that magic optimal discontinuity, optimal unpredictability. And I think we would both agree on clinical grounds that we have typically throughout human development overestimated the capacity of the child to deal with discrepancy. That is, we think he can do more, he can tolerate more discomfort, he can tolerate more anxiety, because he demonstrates that he can. Because of the adaptability that I spoke of earlier, the child will solve almost any problem that you present him with. We've been less sensitive than we might have been to how diminished some of those solutions are. Let me give you an example which came to my attention only today. A first-grader working on his worksheet recognizes that some of his peers look at other people's papers and will copy from them. And in order to forestall that, he fakes an answer with his pencil so that if anybody is copying they will copy the wrong one. Now that's a very elegant solution. One might say, "What an advanced child," but it is so primitive in terms of intellectual achievement and social relations that I am very much distressed by it. So here we have a child who is otherwise vulnerable to all sorts of anxieties (he's a very anxious child as a matter of fact) but he has made this kind of very primitive solution to this complex intellectual and social problem.

What we have not done a good job at . . . is recognition of what the problems are and what it is we want the child to be. I've come to realize that many of the problems that pose as technical, many of the problems that pose as normative, are in fact moral, are in fact ethical problems. Just this last term where I've been teaching a course in educational psychology, it struck me that the things we are interested in in the schools are often times questions of goal-setting; they are not how do you get from here to there, but where do you want to go. And developmental psychologists have been almost completely unwilling to make evaluative and goal-setting statements about what a child should be like. And because of their unwillingness to do that in a frank fashion on philosophical and moral and political grounds, we've often had to do it in a way that draws on our knowledge.

That is, instead of saying, "I think children should be socially flexible because I think children should be socially flexible . . ." we try to defend such propositions as though they derive from research. And I think that's the fake that we really have to watch out for. You shouldn't make evaluative statements falsely on the basis of research findings. And second, there is absolutely nothing wrong in making goal-setting statements and evaluative statements and fighting them out on their just philosophical and ethical grounds.

TOM LEVIN

My basic hypothesis is that you cannot educate children away from their society. You cannot educate them against their parents; it's a totally imperialist thing to do. You cannot lay on to a society an education which does not have roots in that society. . . . The Child Development Group of Mississippi was subversive in that it was against black people having their asses kicked around, against being told that the way you educate black children is to put them in a white school, with white textbooks, white teachers, and give them white notions, and tell them that their parents, their families, their culture, had nothing to offer. You destroy the whole chain of humanity when you take a child and say, "Your parents are no good, there are others who are good." You destroy the chain. It can't be.

I don't know what's good for children and I'm a child analyst for years and what I think is good for children is what *I* think is good for children. It's not what is good for children. There's no such answer to that. I know that children *have* to be a part of society. They cannot be treated as something separate from a society that we will protect from what is real in a society—that we will create an artificial setting for. . . . We don't allow kids to face reality, which I think children *need* to grow. I don't want kids brought up in professionally constructed vacuums of the way children are supposed to be. I also think that I'd rather see black kids brought up in what I consider incidental bad practices, in black communities, with black parents

WHAT DO WE KNOW ABOUT CHILDREN?

doing the bringing up, than in a perfect, beautiful Bank Street School in Jackson, Mississippi. I think that a Bank Street School —as beautiful as it might be—in Jackson, Mississippi, would fuck up the kid's minds. And a black school, where the black parents are frequently repressive, not very responsive to certain levels of creativity, would be better in the end if we could keep the kids and the parents invested in each other all the time. We'd move slower, perhaps, for some individual children, but the total movement would be better. My total thing with CDGM was that you cannot separate the children from their parents and anyone who does it is a kidnapper and the penalty for that is murder.

Let's go back to the whole thing about the role of a scientist in child development. I think there are two kinds of child-development scientists today. There are the normative child-development scientists that measure what they see, and chart it, and then say that's what it is. I think that's very destructive. I think it depends upon the sample you get and from that sample you construct something. Also, you can take an experimental environment—the one thing we know about kids is that they deal with challenge—and if you construct a teaching-machine environment for a child, that will be the child's challenge and he will respond to it. Children just deal with challenge. There is no innate good in children; there is no innate bad in children. There is only something which is beyond that—there is innate growth, there's movement, and there's a need to deal with a challenge. What Erikson calls the growth crisis. And it's different at different ages; it's multidetermined. We don't know the dimensions of each. We have certain general things. Yup, we know that when a kid reaches a certain level of muscular development, he deals with the problems of locomotion and mobility. We know that. But we don't know the social aspects of that. We can deal with how it relates to his family at some level—we know overprotective parents, etc.—but we fail to relate it to the social aspects of that child's real life. We tend to relate it to some concept of an ideal world, and that concept of an ideal world is just our own background.

The other type of child-development scientist is the dynamic.

I think they are people who stay out of schools because schools teach normative. I guess that is part of the foible of being human. We want to know; we want to predict what can happen; we want some course. A dynamic child-development theory would have to deal with anxiety that we don't know—to *live* with that anxiety, to really not say, "This is the answer."

I think if I wanted to do something that I thought would help kids most twenty years from now, I'd eradicate all child-development theory. I would allow no writing on it, or, if I did, only to be read and put away in the archives. We don't know. Our traditional answers are so cluttered with well-meaning, I mean really well-meaning, but it's that we come with too much already determined. I guess I'm part of the people who say, "I don't know anything about child development."

JAMES L. HYMES, JR.

I get very, very impatient with a note that I find going around where people seem to say, "Well, we don't know, we don't know enough." I'm very impressed with the fact that this very year is the fiftieth anniversary of nursery schools in this country . . . that the child-development institutes go back to the late twenties, that there are people in their seventies and eighties who have spent a lifetime in early-childhood education. And I think it's a real mistake to say we don't know anything about kids. I think we do know. . . . We know that a mother-child relationship (I don't mean biological mother) is of prime importance. As a general proposition, I believe very strongly that the overall experiences in early childhood have a major impact on the quality of our adult living.

I think the kind of research that has been done has tended to look at parts of human behavior so that you could get something discrete that could be measured or compared or something of that kind. I think all this over the long haul goes to add up to something at some point, but I'm awfully afraid that the experiences of kids or the experiences of families or the experiences of schools or of centers or communities never, never is the little separate, discrete, isolated item. . . . So while I sometimes sound as though I'm anti-intellectual when I make this kind of a statement, I'm less than enthusiastic about the retrieval of research but am greatly enthusiastic about the retrieval of experiences of sensitive, skilled people who have worked in different settings with people and families. They would be talking subjectively out of their experience where no one would have to say, "You haven't qualified it," or "You didn't do it on a comparative basis," or "What was your end?" I think there's been a kind of resurgence in recent years of some recognition of this sort of experience, but this seems to me to be our greatest need. I don't mean to minimize the other. I want people who want to do that to do it, but I'm not sure the answers as to how you help children, parents . . . are going to come quickly through the small approach. I think we've lost respect for sensitive experience.

MYRTLE MCGRAW

People don't realize that the study of child development is not just mastering information any more than art is a matter of having somebody tell you the techniques. You've got to teach the person to grow along with it and unfortunately both the pedagogical concepts and the theories of learning that we've inherited (I stake my reputation on it) are no good for developing the child during the first three years—or three and a half to four. You've got to begin to think in terms of interrelationships of systems, get stimulus-response out of your thinking ("What do I do," and "Does he do what I want him to do?") and focus on how he does it and what did you do that brings out how he does it. Then I think we could have new guidelines.

JOSEPH REID

When it comes to children, we are in an arena where probably nine-tenths or 95 percent is unknown and 5 percent is known. We are in the beginnings of knowledge. We have tremendous difficulties in communicating with each other—what type of children we are talking about, let alone being able to say, "You do it precisely this way." Whether it is day care or the number of adults you need to care for autistic children, or in another area of child welfare, how you treat successfully the parent who batters his child—in all these areas our knowledge is beginning but it is by no means ending.

PHILIP SAPIR

Philip Sapir can draw upon both his experience as a former staff member of the National Institute of Mental Health and as an executive in The Grant Foundation to offer objective criticisms of child-development theories and research. Few people equal his ability to discern the strengths and weaknesses of the past as well as present day programs for child care, and the failure of research to provide satisfactory underpinnings for such efforts.

You remember there was real excitement that we had really gotten hold of the key theoretical construct that was going to lead us to the solution—you know, the detective-story approach. We had the clue and if we probed deeper and deeper and paid attention to all the fine nuances, we would solve the puzzle. It's been a great disappointment that that approach has led into a morass of finer and finer distinctions and increasingly dubious results and very questionable interpretations and assumptions. It has not come to pass the way it was supposed to. I'm talking about that mental-health, behavioral-science research that had its derivatives from psychodynamic theory, however it was modified by Sears and others.

And maybe this could also be said of learning theory. Again, the idea that there were meaningful laws to be uncovered, and that the more one probed the more there would be a meaningful disclosure of all these nice laws. I think that learning theory and psychoanalytic theory have, to an extent, come a cropper, as any theory will that is applied beyond its proper scope. After a while the facts begin to dispute the theory.

More and more we discover that, as Jerry Kagan and others are now discovering, these things are much more culture-bound, environment-bound, than we have been willing to give credence to. We think we have discovered basic, underlying, fundamental processes. It turns out that they are much more subject to the vagaries of the cultural, social, and even physical and environmental, circumstances—including, certainly, the larger economic and socioeconomic conditions under which people grow and thrive.

The problem with so much of behavioral research that we've been talking about is to get people to really go and see and look and observe. And that doesn't mean in the doctor's office or clinic, but *out*. And this is admittedly difficult. But we still don't know, in fact, what actually happens, for instance, to a deprived child in a disadvantaged family in a ghetto. We don't know what the psychological, nutritional, physical abuse really is. We can only guess at it. Until we actually go and see how many times a child is left alone for hours, or days, or battered, or allowed to suffer from infections that run on, we don't really know. I'm surprised that, after so many years, so little good research has been done on what really goes on within the family setting, the home, let alone the neighborhood, the school, the work setting, and so on. Such an approach means that you don't get nice, quick results which lead to Ph.D.'s and articles in respected journals. And that is a part of that large theme of how the progress of Science, with capital S, is sometimes more determined by the need to earn a living, overidentification with the theories of a given discipline, climbing up the academic ladder, the use of research for the training of students, following the current research fashion of the moment, and so on, than by the pursuit of "science for science's sake," wherever it may lead. My favorite parable is the man (scientist) who is looking for his keys under a nearby lamppost, rather than down the street where he lost them, because, as he explains when asked, "I can't see in the dark."

LEONA BAUMGARTNER   *Trained in bacteriology, pediatrics, and public health, Leona Baumgartner is a former commissioner of health for New York City, where she oversaw the first revision of the sanitary code in forty-five years and helped structure the first municipally financed health research council in the country. She showed great skill in administration and in communicating and working with the mayor, the various boards she was responsible to, and with her staff and constituents. Benjamin Spock was a part-time member of her staff who taught nurses and physicians about the management of behavior problems. Baumgartner later served in the State Department as head of technical assistance programs for underdeveloped nations.*

The thing that worries me is that I think that there are very few answers to emotional problems. You see the places where we've had success are the places where we knew the cause of something and could do something about it. We reduced infant mortality. Now a lot of this has come with an increase in the standard of living, but we've decreased infant and childhood mortality by controlling the common contagious diseases of childhood—polio, measles, pneumonias, everything else. If you took away from our society today the antibiotics—the sulfa drugs, the tranquilizers, the whole series of things like this—you'd have a totally different country. And I think the big successes have come where, epidemiologically speaking, we knew what the cause was and what we could do about it. And I have yet to feel very sure that psychiatry has yet come on that kind of solution. In other words, I think that we've had a tremendous growth of scientific knowledge that led to the control of physical ailments—sometimes too slow but still applied. We don't have the same, in my opinion, body of knowledge in the social sciences.

I think we've still got a big hangover of Puritanism. I recently have written a thing for the New York Academy of Medicine. I went back to take a look at the attitude in Boston and in New

York at the time, in the middle of the nineteenth century, and the puritanical attitudes—if you are godly and if you are clean you some way or other are healthier—come through so clearly. The idea that you could prevent a disease was almost unknown and unthought of. And yet science came along and showed people how to prevent a disease. And I think there's still a lot of that feeling that if you are upright enough some way or another you don't have these social problems. You do.

DAVID SHAKOW

David Shakow considers his contributions to psychology to be in three different spheres: one, maintaining working relationships between psychology and psychiatry; two, advancing the progress of clinical psychology; and three, fostering research in schizophrenia.

One should add to these, however, his unique historical sense of the development of American psychology. This stems from his training at Harvard when the influence of William James was still strong, his experiences in the Worcester child-guidance clinics when they were in their heyday, his dual appointment, at mid-career, at the University of Chicago and the University of Illinois, and finally, his appointment as the director of the Psychology Laboratory in the National Institutes of Health.

Perhaps one of the difficulties in the field is that one doesn't build on another—somebody does a study and you do a study and you don't quite meet exactly the conditions that he did so you can't make a true comparison of your findings because it's so complex. . . . So that when somebody says, "Well, I found this." And the other fellow says, "No, I found this." And then, "Well, we did the same experiment." But when you examine it, you didn't do the same experiment. You may not have had the same motivation. You know the very obvious example of that in the animal field: one fellow lets his rats run directly from a cake onto the maze and the other fellow picks up the rat over here and carries him over to the maze. And the whole difference between their results was apparently in the handling. Here was a rat that had been handled very gently and put in this situation and this one was just dumped into the maze. It's that kind of thing that we haven't been sufficiently subtle about and these are the darned complexities in the human but even in the animal behavioral situation.

MARIAN WRIGHT EDELMAN

Families have to be involved with children if there's going to be any long-range effect and that's still the best vehicle we've got to work with. . . . What we don't know is a lot, but what we do know is that parents are terribly important in children's lives.

Nobody collects facts about kids. What we *don't* know about children in this country is astonishing. It's amazing to me that we ever made a decision that's had *any* good effect. We hired an economist last year . . . and we got him to come down to try to give us a sense of whether we could begin to track down spending on children at the federal level. Well, he spent a couple of months just on child-nutrition programs, and we got as many different answers about what the government had spent last year on child-nutrition programs as there were agencies—including OBM, Agriculture, HEW, OEO. And finally we came back around saying, "When will you guys agree on how much was spent?" And somebody finally admitted that "None of us knows." It's just so hard to begin to put together just *basic* facts about children's programs.

There's a huge catalogue of agencies providing children's services. I'm sure that it is not adequate; and I'm sure nobody really knows. And the question is whether or not Senator Mondale's committee on children might not begin to try to plow through some of that rubbish and come up with just a road map.

HERBERT ZIMILES *Herbert Zimiles speaks frankly and critically in evaluating the role of research in developmental psychology and its deficiencies in focusing on children and their nature. He is a researcher and chairman of the research division of the Bank Street College, which is renowned for its work in early education.*

The whole question of what we are learning from research is a troubling one. It is a question I ask with anger a good deal of the time and I find it particularly frustrating because we are a research division. This is the work we do on a day-to-day basis and yet I have reservations about how useful what we and other people are doing is to people who work with children.

I, like a great many others, tend to emphasize the heuristic value of research. The main benefit that I see from research is in clarifying your thinking about a problem. Somehow, working on a research problem forces you to confront the intricacies of it, it forces you to define what are ambiguous terms, makes you recognize what you thought you knew but really don't know, makes you examine alternative explanations. . . . Where you have a really successful research program the complexity of thinking of the problem at the end of the research program is at a much more advanced stage than it was at the beginning, even though a lot of answers have not been provided. Now, those are some of my values and, on the other hand, it seems to me that a lot of values of the research world militate against this view of the value of research. That is, the payoff in research seems to come from working with very simple questions, keeping things simple . . . working with what is measurable, which right there is enormously restrictive. . . . A successful research project tests a particular hypothesis and gives a seemingly unequivocal answer to it. What I am saying is that in some ways what the research world values is *certainty*. There seems to be an intolerance of ambiguity and, perhaps more important, an impatience with theory, with conjecture. And yet, from my point of view, what we need is an expanding theoretical structure, a greater appetite for dealing with complexity and a gradual elaboration of the complexity of our ideas about children.

I think that child-development researchers, like most research psychologists, deal with glimpses of children and glimpses, I think, don't tell you very much. Our whole experimental code, or methodology, is based upon sampling. The whole notion that it is possible to infer the total from a few fragments, I think, is a questionable assumption, and it means that your definition of the whole is based upon a summation of the observation of fragments, which may be extremely inaccurate. Now, the field is changing and becoming more sophisticated but I am still not satisfied and I think we have a long way to go.

Up until about fifteen years ago, there was not a single textbook in the field of developmental psychology which betrayed any kind of understanding of what children were about. The textbooks were literally organized in terms of topics studied by researchers, and they were simply compilations of glimpses made by different people, and when the author talked about a particular facet of child development the whole discussion consisted of the recitation of findings, most of which were unrelated to each other and which told you very little about the total creature that was used as a subject. And, indeed, I think . . . for example, if somebody came to a developmental psychologist who had written a textbook and said, "I am going to have to deal with children, I am going to have to live with them, I am going to have to work with them, where in this book can I get a really clear notion of what a three-year-old is like, or an eight-year-old is like?" the answer would have been, "There is no place." Literally nobody who was a researcher seemed to have a clear notion of the total child and the nature of the interaction of the parts that make up the psychic nature of the child. Until the Stone and Church book [*Childhood and Adolescence: A Psychology of the Growing Person,* 1957] came out—I think to me that was really a landmark and it was a book, of course, that received a lot of criticism by the researchers for not documenting enough what it was talking about—I knew of no textbook that even remotely provided a clear picture of what a child is like.

There is no question but that Piaget's ideas, the rebirth of interest in Piaget, made it possible for psychologists to begin to talk about psychological constructs which were not directly observable and to act as though it is not just what is there on the surface that is important. I think that through Piaget, and later Bruner and other translators of Piagetian notions, a much more sophisticated and believable and understandable set of ideas about how thought develops has come on the scene and I think that the printed word about the nature of development is infinitely better now than it was twenty years ago.

ALFRED BALDWIN *Baldwin is a pioneer in developmental psychology and is in a position to analyze its historical development and its significance, particularly in relation to child psychology. He shares an interest in ecological psychology with Urie Bronfenbrenner. He is professor of psychology at the University of Rochester.*

I think what I see most missing in psychology, developmental psychology along with other kinds, is a real analysis of the child's environment and of his interaction with people who are important to him. It seems to me we've had so much experimental material of how children *might* be influenced by various kinds of circumstances but so little data on whether or not, in real life, these circumstances arise, whether the kinds of reinforcement schedules that presumably could establish a very high response rate in rats, whether children ever actually receive those. It seems to me that child psychology has been—I think very healthily—influenced by behavioristic theory, and learning theory, and social learning theory, but that what is *missing* from the contributions of those theoretical points of view is the way the actual environment is structured. Now I think that we could certainly take *that* theoretical point of view and look at natural environment in terms of reinforcement schedules and contingencies. And some people are trying to, but not many. . . . I think, in a sense, I feel as if I have become a psychological ecologist.

EDWARD ZIGLER

My reading of the history of child development is that there is so much of a swinging pendulum effect in it. Santayana, I guess, said it, "Those who cannot remember the past are condemned to repeat it," and that is so true in the child area. The environmental mystique was itself a reaction against the Gessellian era, with its emphasis on maturation and the implicit notion of the fixed IQ and hereditary factors and so forth and so on. And then it went too far in the direction of, "Gee, the child is a kind of empty organism that we can program in any way that we like," with not enough respect for biology and not enough respect for autonomous factors. Now we see a reaction setting in against the environmental mystique on the part of the hereditarians, the Jensens, and a new kind of emphasis on genetics. And unless people have a sense of history to know that, "Gee, we've come this way before," I don't think we're ever going to have a generation of child-development workers who try to finally move on from these extreme positions and begin dealing with the real complexities of child development—begin appreciating all the factors and do away with these simplistic approaches to the child.

4 Can Scientific Knowledge Help Frame Our Social Policies for Children?

We are often told indeed that even the experts do not know how to deal with the problems that now threaten worldwide disaster: that 'all the facts are not yet in,' that more research must be done, and more reports written. By all means let us have more research. But that must not be allowed to become a trap, an excuse for endlessly putting off action. We already know enough to begin to deal with all our major problems: nuclear war, overpopulation, pollution, hunger, the despoliation of the planet. The present crisis is a crisis, not of information, but of policy.

George Wald, Harvard University, 1975

The whole controversy of the relevance and usefulness of what we have learned about children in planning for them came to a head as the Johnson administration sought to create the Great Society. In waging its "war on poverty," the government called on the specialists in child development—psychologists, pediatricians, psychiatrists, and social workers—to help plan new programs for the "disadvantaged children" whose plight had been brought to national attention by the migrations from the South to urban centers and by the civil rights movement. As a result, new concepts and organizations became an important influence in the lives of many poor children. Head Start, Home Start, open classroom education, Follow Through, became household words, and day care became a high-priority issue.

This section and the next are devoted to a discussion of just how useful scientific knowledge has proved to be in the formulation of programs relating to children. The high faith in man's ability to change his circumstances through scientific knowledge and governmental resources which characterized the 1960s has given way to disillusionment in the seventies. Today the prevailing mood seems to be more nearly that "nothing works." In moments of discouragement I, too, have felt that much of our research has led only to confusion, contradiction, and paralysis. In fairness to the scientists and for the benefit of those who wish to avail themselves of their knowledge, a realistic assessment of present capabilities in planning for children and at least a quick review of some of the things that have been accomplished because of scientific findings is attempted here.

MARIAN WRIGHT EDELMAN

No social scientists would agree on what the early child-development literature shows or on what would make a difference. . . . I'll never again be intimidated by academics. It's all gamesmanship. And it's very hard to sit there and not say, "So what?" I mean, why is this important to debate these narrow issues of no importance? And how does that help with Monday morning trying to help the folk out there who need help. The child developmentalists don't know what they want; they're cautious. When you begin to talk about the issues involved in trying to frame legislation, they haven't thought about those issues in real people's terms. . . . They don't know how to take a position because they don't know whether something is going to work in terms in which they analyze—which is not direct services, is not meals, is not health exams, is not happiness. It's, you know, IQ games, or it's something that you can show to a legislature that produces results in your concrete terms, that says that is a better way to spend money than this— "Spend it on revenue sharing." So it's that their framework is so different from what real people have to deal with.

The academics simply don't understand Washington, they don't understand policy, they don't understand choices, they don't understand real people and tomorrows. I'd like to be able to have social-science data that supports our point of view. I could try to put together a committee of those people to come in and testify that the Child Development bill * is a terrific thing to pass. But the other side can produce as many people on the other side and I think we're not going to be able to justify the passage or nonpassage of this bill based on social science. I think in my center it would be more harmful than helpful. It's just going to make everybody feel that much more uncertain about whether it's important. I think we have to stick with what we know is concrete and is common sense, like health, like nutrition, like just having kids in a safe, decent place when their parents are going to work. The best argument I think for a good system is that we've got a very bad one already that we're going to deal with next Monday morning. You just stay away from these nebulous kinds of social-science bases. I think we all ought to support research. We ought to know more. I think we'll know more as we proceed, but I'm not clear how

* A bill being considered by Senator Mondale for introduction in the Congress in 1976–77.

we'll ever know more if we don't have some programs from which we can proceed to evaluate.

I think we just have to begin to try to start a debate on how we look at programs. And maybe what I'm saying is basically a kind of accountability and a kind of evaluation that ought to be the basis for our deciding whether programs should exist—whether the parents like them or think it's important, or think it's good for their kids. And that's as important as what Shep White says about that program.

DAVID ELKIND

We've had a lot of data about the impact of early-childhood stimulation, and literally hundreds of thousands—thousands of studies in early childhood, trying to improve IQ. You know, people tried to give the impression that new findings from Piaget and all these people gave you the impetus for Head Start, but I never saw it; that is, a lot of this data we had had for a long time and could be interpreted in just the opposite way. The scientific base for those programs was, I thought, very weak because for every argument that one could make from data for Head Start one could argue just the opposite. For example, on the Bloom stuff that half the child's IQ is attained by age four—well, it's also true that 80 percent is attained by age eight after he's had a very small amount of formal education so one could say that the child makes greatest educational growth when he's not receiving any formal education and therefore we ought to cut out formal education because he learns most without it. You could say that or you could say, why not wait a couple of years; when he's eight he'll have 80 percent of his intellectual potential and he'll learn things much more rapidly and quickly. One could make, I think, a solid argument for this but no one chose to interpret it that way. People chose to interpret it another way. I would say, if you had to say which came first, my guess is that social policy often dictates what will be taken from the literature and emphasized and what will not be acknowledged. I've seen this in personal ways: if you don't go according to the party line of the power structure, you get neglected because you don't fit in. So I guess I'm pretty cynical about impact of research on policy. I rather think policy determines what's selected.

CHARLES P. GERSHENSON

My impression is that, for the most part, research in the field of child development was not oriented, not organized, not directed, toward planning nor was it directed toward planning programs. As we keep saying, it was to satisfy the inner needs of the investigator, his curiosity, and a lot of it was academically based and oriented. And, as we've come to realize now, it reflected our culture, you can call it our biases, our perception. We were living and are living in a country which, until very recently, never did planning, either at the local level or at the national level, unlike the centrally planned economies that you find. And my UNICEF experience has shown me the difference between what goes on in this country and the other countries. We never plan what we want to achieve with children in the next five years: how many would be in school, at what reading level, achieving what. It was only in the latter half of the sixties that planning began to take on a more organized effort.

So, when you look at most research you would say and I would say that most research had very little impact upon services or planning. As a matter of fact when a social issue arose the cry was the lack of data, the lack of relevant research, the lack of relevant information. It's only recently that the social scientists, the academicians, have become conscious of the needs of research for planning. For the most part during the sixties we were unprepared with our knowledge base to meet with the social issues with which we were presented. So, in essence, we used the minimal knowledge we had and also we were more like informed lay people than professionals in recommending programs.

ORVILLE G. BRIM, JR.

The Advisory Committee on Child Development, which is in the Assembly of Behavioral and Social Sciences of the National Academy of Science, was set up in 1972 to take stock of what we knew and what a group of professional child-development students and practitioners would recommend as policies for the nation. And on that committee were people like Bronfenbrenner, Richmond, and others. We've been meeting off and on for about a year and a half and we had such difficulties in pulling it together that I think it's a good point of entry into discussing some of the matters involved. With reference to the use of child-development research and its influence on public policy, we examined the White House Conference Report of 1909 and all the ones since then (the Joint Commission on Mental Health of Children, and other major studies), and a substantial number —like 90 percent—of the recommendations made in 1909 are still suitable today for the commission to reassert. The fact is that probably the majority of this 90 percent has still not been acted upon in any way by a policy body. So, this implies two things: there is a continuity in what professionals believe is desirable for child-care practices over the past sixty years; and secondly, that the children of the United States do not seem to be an important political constituency. . . . Thus, it's somewhat depressing to serve on another national committee with lots of experts to develop guidelines for the nation on research and activities for policy. Rather than attempt to hand in another set of items without priorities, we said, "Why not just run off another copy of the 1909 White House Report, put the committee's signature on it, and hand that in?"

There was the feeling that reports should have a factual basis describing what's known about children and then the policies stated in that. And Harold Stevenson, the chairman, and I and some other people met with a group on the west coast and elsewhere to get a quick overview of what we know about children. . . . The other argument was, "Why not just cite the existence of the Jones Carmichael handbooks and their revisions —800 or 900 pages of what we know out of psychology primarily—plus handbooks on pediatrics and the like, and say this is what's known?" Well, the thought was . . . you have to summarize in some broad sweep. But that turned out to be not the way to do it because we came out with such general platitudes, such as children developed better under conditions of autonomy and nurturance and support—that kind of level—that it became fatuous. So the committee decided not to summarize it or even state anything about what is known about child development, which I think is an interesting point. We've gotten to the point where so much is known that you can't summarize it, and yet the broad outlines turn out to be, as I say, kind of modern-day common sense. So the report goes definitely to policy implications.

The failure to make more use of our child-development knowledge in public-policy formation stems both from the familiar problem of transfer of information to the policy sector and also from the character of the information that we have to offer. It seems to me that there has been a missing component in our understanding of child development. I conceptualize the research as being concerned primarily with the analysis and description of characteristics of the child, whether cognitive or affective or interpersonal, or with developmental stages and the developmental norms, with maturational effects and . . . conceptualization of motivation, of linguistics and the like—in essence, analysis, conceptualization, of a child's personality broadly conceived. And we also have studies of what I'm now calling "microstructural" effects—fine-grain analyses of the influence of a particular variability of parents' behavior on a child's personality. This includes work done on variations in weaning and toilet-training schedules . . . the effects of father absence, the effects of maternal deprivation, the effects of different kinds of teacher-pupil interactions, the effects of having an older same sex or opposite sex sib.

One level above this is a "meso-structural" level, or middle level of influence, which has to do with the studying of the characteristics of types of families, or types of child-care institutions, types of schools, but without looking at individual variability within such systems. That is, is the extended family better than the nuclear family for certain types of child care? Are large versus small classrooms important for children? Now, it's been difficult to generate propositions about these relationships which provide for points of intervention and change because if one were to say, for instance, that an extended-family system has more desirable consequences for children than a nuclear-family system, the question then becomes, how do you generate an extended-family system or the facsimile thereof? That kind of intervention or policy-planning question forces you back to consideration of the next order of determinants of the situation, namely, what influences are there that generate different kinds of family systems, school systems, day-care systems, health-delivery systems, and the like?

We are led back to consideration of economic influences, of historical factors, cultural factors, sociological, political-science factors. For instance, it leads us back to questions of income-distribution and income-maintenance policies and . . . into questions of the effects of the race discrimination/social stratification system on different kinds of family operations. It leads into questions of values of intimacy and affective response that young men and women want from marriage . . . which make them very tied to a nuclear rather than an extended family system. It's not only my own thinking about this which has come up in this foundation, the same is occurring in Urie Bronfenbrenner's work in ecology in which his confrontation with the kinds of questions asked by policy makers leads him back into these "macrostructural" determinants, or settings, of child-care institutions. In like manner Ken Keniston's forthcoming [Carnegie] Council report will emphasize such major institutional determinants rather than little interventions.

What I am trying to do, what other people are trying to do,

what I think will inevitably happen, is the development of research linking these kinds of macrostructural policies on the intermediate institutions and eventually on children. And that's what I see is going to happen in the next stage in the legislative use of child development.

Let's return to the income distribution as an example. We have information now suggesting that the participation of young children in group settings, day-care settings so to speak, preschool settings, without their mother or father, under good auspices, is not detrimental to the child's growth as we thought ten or fifteen years ago. And indeed for parents of poorer background it's often beneficial. The centers are able to offer more than the parents can at home. Partly this is Head Start data, partly it is parent-training data and the like. So the question then becomes, how do you get the kind of quality day-care institutions which research has shown to be benign to the child rather than detrimental day-care institutions, where there will be supervision and where the quality of the personnel is at least paraprofessional. Now the argument that, say, Mary Keyserling would make is that without federal supervision, strong federal supervision, standard setting, the quality of the day-care units, when passed on to some of our less enlightened and poorer states and local communities, would be custodial; that costs and standards would be cut, that children would be brutalized, that there would be ethnic and racial segregation of institutions, and the like. Harold Watts, on the other hand, argues that if you go that way rather than allow parents a free choice through income redistribution to do this, the cost to the government would be too large to be able to support adequate care, there would not be enough innovation, the well-to-do middle class would take advantage . . . and would have good institutions.

This is a major issue involving something like 4 to 6 million children and maybe $10 billion each year for the foreseeable future—I'd say over the next twenty-five years. To start on one policy or the other policy makes it difficult to retract and commits the country to a trajectory which may be good or bad. Research, very substantial research, on an experimental basis on the consequences of these two alternative policies ideally should be undertaken before the nation is committed. That's the kind of research that I think we're going to see more of.

JULE SUGARMAN   *Sugarman is well acquainted with the workings of bureaucracies and the dilemmas of bureaucrats. He has served in various agencies of the federal and municipal governments and was a working director of Head Start and the Office of Child Development in Washington, D.C. Most recently, he has become a close associate of the mayor of Atlanta in administering that city.*

I basically believe that it is terribly important to research programs and to evaluate programs. I am sorely disappointed, though, in the caliber of information which is available, in the unwillingness of researchers to deal with the questions which are important questions to us as administrators, and perplexed with the inability of experts to agree with one another. I've sat through I don't know how many hours, with really solid professional people arguing about details and not being able to agree with one another, and what that brings you to at the bottom line is that no expert will acknowledge that the studies of another expert are valid. So when you turn to them and say, "How much confidence can I as an administrator put in what you've done," the answer is, "None—we don't have enough information, we haven't studied this enough. You'll just have to make your own judgments." So I would say essentially that during the entire time that I operated in Head Start or in the child-development field with HEW, I don't think there was an instance in which I was able to rely on any scientific study as a guide to policy.

WILLIAM KESSEN

In the fifties and in the sixties we oversold ourselves or were oversold . . . in all the child fields, but certainly in the areas of cognitive and social development and exquisitely in the field called learning. People expected us to have answers which simply don't exist. So that there were necessarily disappointments and frustrations from practitioners, whether educators or clinicians. And I think we are still suffering from that and will continue to do so, partly because we continue to raise expectations excessively, and partly because it is going to take a long time before any of the answers are available. We haven't developed the experimental procedures, we haven't developed the empirical ways of attacking these problems which will be appropriate. I think we have some of the right attitudes now, but it is going to be a long time before anybody can go to Congress, or to the people at the National Institute of Education and say, "This is what you should do to try and solve these problems." It's easy to understand why some of us have preferred to do studies which can be defended on their academic, scholarly, and intrinsic basis, and been a little bit chary about jumping into these areas of practical application. I'm so struck by this in the first grade. The things I can share with the teacher I am working with have relatively little to do with anything I know as a psychologist. I know that I have to deal with my own feeling about children and some of the things I've learned from working with them—but to tag it as expert knowledge is to mislead everyone.

SHELDON WHITE

I believe that psychology has had an important social impact, even though psychology is very primitive. I regard psychology as essentially like alchemy. There are important resemblances between psychology and medieval alchemy. We keep promising people we're going to turn lead into gold; we can't do it; we don't even begin to know how to do it. And in time that probably won't be the important question. We're very primitive, and yet, I think, because of the complexity of modern society, we are necessary.

People in a society like ours, whether they like it or not, are psychologists. If a man runs a program in Washington, if he is in the bureaucracy, having to do with people, everyday he has to ask himself questions which are basically the questions the social scientists ask themselves. Now, we don't know the answers, and he doesn't know the answers, but we can ask the questions a little better than he can and we are a little less confused about what the general issues are. We can help him, not by telling him what the answers are, but by at least sort of getting him to address the issues in a slightly different way.

I have no problems about relevance of the field, although I don't believe this field is going to have a magic bullet in the next hundred years or so. And I do believe we waste a lot of time. I think a lot of what goes on in the field is ritualism. I don't know how much there has to be to have a substantial field but I think a lot of it is junk. I don't know how much of it you have to pay for.

The Congressmen are now getting educated the hard way about what we don't know, and I hope a little bit about what we might know a little bit about—and we are going to get educated the hard way about the questions they want us to answer, as opposed to the questions we like them to ask us. I believe what we are getting in our time is basically . . . a kind of estimation of, let's say, what the resources are in this funny kind of child-development and social-policy axis.

I think politicians have to learn what it is that academics really do as opposed to what academics would like them to *think* they do. And academics have to learn . . . what it is that will *really help* kids as opposed to what it is that will really look good back home at the campus.

JUDITH MILLER *Judith Miller was a legislative assistant to Senator Prouty and an assistant to Elliot Richardson when he was Secretary of HEW. She is now the director of the Health Staff Seminar of George Washington University for employees of federal agencies and others. She has had firsthand experience with expert witnesses and speaks with authority about their usefulness to legislators.*

People in the field don't know how to give input into the legislative process. People doing work in child development are terrible. The very few who are interested in legislation come to the Hill with reams and reams of data which they won't net out. If you ask them the conclusions for legislative implications, they don't want to be quoted; they don't want to make a hypothesis on what is the best way to write a bill—they just say, "Well, you're the legislative type, you make the decision." No legislative aide has the time to read through those reams of materials. Or they come up not understanding the legislative process at all. They come in with information when it is too late. They literally don't understand how a bill is written.

JULIUS RICHMOND *As a former director of Head Start, as well as a pediatric clinician, teacher, and researcher, Julius Richmond has been faced frequently with the need to support research and to try to act on its data. His opinions have cogency because of his unique experiences in both federal agencies and universities. A man of many talents and responsibilities, he is director of the Judge Baker Guidance Center in Boston, psychiatrist-in-chief at the Children's Hospital Medical Center, and professor of child psychiatry and human development and professor of preventive and social medicine at Harvard.*

I guess I have been disappointed over the years in the resistance of people who have scientific knowledge in the professions of child development to move toward the implementation of programs to improve the lives of children. Generally, the reasoning of many of the research workers that I have been in contact with runs something like the following: "We don't know for sure that what we are recommending will produce all of the desired effects and until we know for sure we should remain aloof from trying to implement programs or from trying to make recommendations." I think that that position doesn't make sense. Since people in communities, and particularly decision-makers whether they are in public office or in private agencies or wherever, look to the people who have professional competence to make judgments about what is a more likely direction in which we ought to go, for people who are most knowledgeable to walk away from making recommendations for programs for children seems to me to be inappropriate. And as a consequence, what I think I would like to spend most of my time on from here on . . . is moving much more toward the application of the knowledge that we have in more effective, hopefully more creative, ways. And I don't mean this to be taken in any antiresearch way. I'm not suggesting that we don't need more knowledge but I think there are many potentially creative ways that we can apply the knowledge that we already have to try to improve the development of our children.

EDWARD ZIGLER

As much as we don't know about children (we are the ones that certainly know the most), if we don't make ourselves available in social policy for children I think it's going to remain bad. I have been surprised for years and years by the reluctance of good people to assume a public position. Not only do they not do it because they are apathetic towards it, but it almost has a negative valence for them; it is somehow prostituting oneself to enter the public arena. I think that until we do away with that kind of thinking, the children in this nation are simply not going to profit by the best input that our leaders in child development can offer.

I think that we certainly know more about children than we're using—that's the problem. Let's certainly use our knowledge in those areas where we don't have complete knowledge, but we simply can't wait, where we have to make our most educated guesses.

ROBERT ALDRICH *A pediatrician by training, Aldrich left a professorship at the University of Washington to become the first director of the National Institute of Child Health and Human Development.*

He returned to the university after a few years in federal service, with new convictions about the roles and responsibilities of the social, behavioral, and medical sciences. He is presently continuing to pursue his interests in education and in the preparation of persons in the health sciences for social change as a vice-president of the University of Colorado.

I went to the National Institutes of Health and spent two years during the Kennedy administration when the Institute of Child Health and Human Development was set up. That was a turning point, as far as I was concerned, in my career because it was the first time I could see how much we knew and how little of the known was being applied. It's so obvious from the federal position that the distribution of what we know . . . to the people who need this information, this help, is blocked. There's just a huge bottleneck there; there's just very little going through this. As the new knowledge accumulates and gets larger and larger and larger, the little loophole it goes through to be utilized just doesn't seem to change very much. So, when I got back to the university, it seemed to me that this was the place to work—to try to break that bottleneck up as much as possible. I felt that the social sciences, behavioral sciences, were one of the kinds of hammers you could use. . . . I mean, this really had to do with how you get people to accept new information, how you get the medical profession to see, and how to translate something they know into service to people; how to get it out of the laboratory into the political system so it can be distributed, or into the service system so it can be distributed.

KENNETH KENISTON

We ourselves have been determined to limit our calls for more research. There clearly is more research needed, but it seems, to me at least, that we really know how to do a lot of things. We could make a lot of difference with what we already know and we really don't need to wait around for fifteen years of demonstration projects or evaluated research to be able to help children. Furthermore it seems to me that a lot of research ought to be concurrently evaluated action research. Instead of, you know, running Head Start for five years and saying, "Oops, it didn't work," we ought to commit ourselves to certain goals, constantly do research as we go but not with the goal of deciding whether the program is a failure or not but with the goal of trying to correct its failures and make it work if it does not work.

I don't think research per se leads automatically to policy. In this country we have done a lot of very exhaustive research in a number of areas ranging from parent-child and family interactions to out-of-family care, to children's health needs and so on. This research can falsify myths, it can disabuse people of incorrect ideas. Insofar as policy is based on incorrect ideas one wants to modify the policy. But it is essential that policy include, besides facts, information, and scientific knowledge, some notions of goals and targets and values and aspirations. Scientific knowledge alone is never enough to make policy. I was talking, a couple of years ago, with someone in Congress. It was just after Kagan had come up with his report on Guatemalan children implying that it didn't make much difference what you did in the first year and so on; it was after Armour had come up with his finding that integration did not make much difference; it was after Jencks had come up with his report that schools don't make much difference. This legislator said, jokingly: "My God, for years we have been trying to work with these people, we have been basing our work on them. But now the first thing I would do is to blow up Harvard." He felt double-crossed in that he had been trying to use research that showed that early damage is hard to remedy, on the importance of integration, on the importance of schooling. But now academics were saying—I think prematurely—that the earlier research was all wrong. Some politicians seem to be smarter than most of us academics are.

WALTER MONDALE

We had, in the middle of our effort to try to pump some more money into Title I and so on, and into our equal education effort, to try to sort out the factors of discrimination and so on that were impeding the progress of children. We were visited with Moynihan reports that said, "Nothing works." Christopher Jencks's book was sold that said that neither antidiscrimination or money helped. I remember Moynihan being quoted about one Harvard report saying, "Well, what we found is that instead of putting money into education, just give them $300 so that they can go visit the ocean." Now, I would like to see them visit the ocean, I don't put that down, but the underlying point is that, "Nothing works, social programs are all failures, they are all ripoffs and therefore drop them." And the net result of those studies is less money, less attention, and essentially a resignation by Americans toward the whole concept of equal justice through strategies that equip children with the tools they need to succeed. I was very resentful and I am now because, frankly, I think they were selling books and the kids are paying the price right now.

HERBERT ZIMILES

The research psychologist flies the flag of science so high and so proudly that he succeeds in intimidating his audience, including the politicians sometimes. They delude themselves into thinking that they have scientific evidence for their statements and as a result they can bring to bear pressure, they can release funds, which nonresearcher professionals who work more in isolation and who can't trumpet their scientific background cannot do. You take the whole early-childhood education in the Head Start era—there's been a veritable revolution in this country. Whereas ten years ago education for children under the age of five or six in most of the states was not available except for the most privileged, now it's come to be widely accepted as enormously valuable. Research psychologists were given the most powerful posts in universalizing early-childhood education, even though I believe that they knew virtually nothing about the field and where they started their own programs started very poor programs.

But by describing their really conventional and lackluster programs within an experimental framework, and by accompanying their descriptions with piles of data (much of it irrelevant and invalid), they had the muscle to persuade policymakers. And now, preschool is widespread.

I think that there are some psychologists who know the most —or are among those who know the most—about what is the best for children. Their voices should be heard. But people with such knowledge and experience are shockingly rare. I think one of the things that is missing is that very few psychologists can say, "This and this is needed by children because this and this happens if you don't do that and that." Instead, we are so empirical that all that most of us can say is, "We have found that this produces that outcome and that doesn't." But what is needed, I think, are briefs—reasoned, elaborated through speculative statements of why one particular form of treatment should be used as opposed to another. "If you do this, that will be affected in this way which in turn will adversely affect this," and so forth and so on. But because theoretical speculation is so alien to us and sustained observation of children is rare, very few psychologists can write a good brief and that's what I think we have to be trying to do for legislators and those foundation people, educators, people who have the power to influence how agencies that work with children will function.

But right now my problem is that I don't trust most psychologists' judgment on these matters, and I think that they are not capable of writing these briefs. Most graduate students are trained mainly in fancy methodology and are taught to suspect theoretical speculation. This is what has to be changed.

ALBERT J. SOLNIT

Albert Solnit is a psychoanalyst with firsthand knowledge of social science. In his capacity as director of the Yale Child Study Center he reaffirms the traditional roles of the social scientist as observer and responsible reporter of our society and its activities rather than inviting them to be more active agents for direct change. His words are a reminder that progress may be made not only by change in professional function but by enlarging the field's traditional scope and depth.

I don't think social scientists have had much of an impact on attitudes towards children and families. I think that perhaps their greatest contribution on the whole has been to reflect on what is happening rather than to influence it and to bring it about. It is always very difficult to know which study, which report, which published or spoken or dramatized message really does change the attitude of policy-makers towards children and their families. So that, on the whole, social scientists, I think, have been unsuccessful in bringing about change. There are some exceptions, but I am not sure that those exceptions warrant a change in my generalization.

We are surprised, Professor Joseph Goldstein, Dr. Anna Freud and I, that our little book, *Beyond the Best Interests of the Child* [1973], seems to have had the impact it has on the courts and on some of the legislators of this country and in England as well. Also it is being used in some of the European countries. Perhaps the social scientist is like any other contributor when knowledge has reached a point where it's time for a certain question or a certain formulation to be offered. If one is fortunate enough to be there at the time with the clear message that society is ready for, one can think that one has had an impact. I do have a belief that knowledge moves ahead slowly, step by step, and that each of us may contribute a little bit. But very few can say they had a major impact on what might have happened.

I think the social scientist can make a very important contribution by being an excellent mirror of what we are doing, and by trying to make not a long-term but short-term predictions of what will happen as our mirror reflects what our theory and methods show. I would say we must mobilize a kind of reflection . . . a kind of multifaceted picture of what's happening to the family, not only in the United States but all over the world, because the family is not just a contrivance or an artificial institution. It is something that arises out of the way in which people need each other and count on each other. I believe the family is changing rapidly and I think social scientists should keep track of it and hold up that mirror for us to see because when we understand what is happening, I think we are better able to engage in useful political action.

5 Have Social Scientists Changed Our Attitudes and Behavior toward Children?

The most imaginative and powerful movements in the history of science have arisen not from plan and not from compulsion, but from the spontaneous enthusiasm and curiosity of capable individuals who had the freedom to think about the things they considered interesting.

Warren Weaver

JOAN COSTELLO *On the basis of her work in administering psychological tests to children and in evaluating the results of tests, particularly those relating to intelligence, Joan Costello has mixed feelings about tests and their educational benefits. She is assistant professor of psychology at the Yale Child Study Center, and formerly assistant director of the Carnegie Council on Children, a study commission under the direction of Kenneth Keniston.*

Working in schools I became very aware that testing contributed something to American kids that I can't put together with my dislike of testing. A lot of children whom teachers used to call dumb, because they were dark in color or they smelled, had test scores to demonstrate that they had strengths and skills. Those scores, at least for some, introduced a kind of objectivity into the education of children that I guess we didn't have before. I remember my mother saying that as a fifth-grader a teacher told her: "No Wop can ever learn arithmetic," and my father saying that Irish kids were not expected to do well in school. I knew coming up that kids couldn't depend on the good will of teachers to develop their potential. Tests were there and my parents counted on that. If I had any ability, they believed the tests would protect me from the biases of teachers. But there is another side—a more disturbing one. I am dismayed at what's happened with tests. The whole history of how they were developed reveals their use to exclude people rather than include them. At the same time I am aware of how many children of poor and minority ethnic groups had a chance at higher education because of tests. Family and wealth did not count as much once you could demonstrate on a test that you had something "upstairs." Intelligence testing—achievement testing—too have made a mixed contribution to the educational research field.

One other child development research contribution is quite recent and that is the discovery that before they come to school children do learn things that are important for the rest of their lives. The notion that kids shouldn't be taught anything before they come to school because it will mess up the reading program is not heard that much anymore. It's only since the preschool programs of the sixties that teachers have been convinced that learning does not begin in first grade. I guess one could not call that a contribution of research but rather a happenstance of preschool programs. But certainly in the last ten or fifteen years research has flooded the popular media (and teachers and most people don't read anything but popular media) with the notion that learning begins at birth, or begins very early anyway, and that children are always absorbing things and using experiences and so on. Even the research about mother-child interaction and about social-class differences has its dark side. We think in terms of the social biases that we grow up with and that has probably done a lot of harm by implying that since what happens to children is a function of what their parents and other people do with them, it is then entirely in the power of parents or teachers to consciously and deliberately shape their destinies. I think in the common mind and in the mind of practicing teachers and others . . . the notion until recently was that a young child was a sort of genetically determined, Gesellian child that unfolded with whatever endowment it had. As long as you took good physical care of it and treated it well that was all there was to it. Certainly the research in the last ten or fifteen years—much of it in cognitive development—has shifted that view. Now, people are aiming to increase kids' IQs and teach them to read at age two. I guess no gain is without its loss, no research entirely free of the social context in which it is concerned or applied.

J. MCVICKER HUNT

At the end of World War II René Spitz appeared on the scene with his motion pictures of child-rearing in two institutions. One was a hospital, an institution in a place that Spitz would never name, and the other was a prison where the mothers could interact with their children—also a place that Spitz would never name. Even though Sam Pinneau pointed up a great many discrepancies in Spitz's articles on hospitalism and anaclitic depression, his criticisms failed to inhibit the impact of Spitz on both theory and practice. I believe this was because Spitz's movies were exceedingly effective and convincing. It was very clear that these babies in the hospital were indeed retarded. They created sympathy. Spitz interpreted these effects to result from a lack of a one-to-one relationship between the infant and the mother or mother surrogate. As a consequence, multiple mothering became an anathema in psychoanalytical circles and outside psychoanalytical circles as well. Institutions for infants also became anathema and psychoanalytic psychiatrists joined social workers to get laws passed in, I believe, every state in the union outlawing orphanages, especially for infants under two. As a consequence we have no orphanages for young babies in America, or very few of them. There was one in Washington, D.C., that operated up until a very few years ago.

In the place of orphanages there began to develop foster homes. Unfortunately, I'm afraid we simply don't know what's happening in a large share of foster homes and there is some question whether it's any better for the children than what could happen in a good orphanage. One of the values of a good orphanage was that it provided a place where child-rearing could be studied. I've had to go to Tehran and Greece in order to get access to such institutions and I'm happy to say that both the audiovisual enrichment and the human enrichment, in which we taught the caretakers what to do, has been very effective in fostering the development of object construction and vocal imitation. The babies in the Tehran orphanage who have been under this program are showing progress that is approximately equal to that of home-reared infants from middle-class families.

Nevertheless, it must be said that René Spitz was very effective in making a major reform in the fashion in which children were reared and in what psychiatrists, social workers, and child psychologists believe is important in the early years or in the early months of life.

ORVILLE G. BRIM, JR.

One thing that has happened in the past three or four years is the great growth of child advocacy by public interest or *pro bono* law programs—like Children's Defense Fund, Mental Health Law Project, the New York Civil Liberties Union, and others. Now, that's not exactly a direct transfer of knowledge to the policymakers; the situation is one in which information gathered about children and about child development is marshaled by the advocacy group to demonstrate that children are being deprived of constitutional or statutory rights and the use of child-development data therefore is to force a judicial ruling, or administrative ruling, to accord with the law. So that's a new use, so to speak, of child-development data—not new, in essence, because it was also the case with the desegregation decision during the fifties and there were other uses before this. But to have this used to such extent is new. That's a rather different use of child-development information than one we might envisage, which is to have the new information generate new institutions or new laws and new statutes as our knowledge grows.

NICHOLAS HOBBS *This psychologist wears many hats. Former provost of Vanderbilt University, he is currently director of the Center for the Study of Families and Children of the Vanderbilt Institute for Public Policy Studies. The excerpt that follows presents the genesis of his concepts about institutional programs for the education, psychotherapy, and rehabilitation of mentally retarded or emotionally and behaviorally disturbed children.*

The way I got really concerned with institutional forms for children was in about 1953 or 1954. The Southern Regional

Educational Board in Atlanta asked me to direct a study of mental-health resources for training and research in the South. One of the things that was just startling was the despair about children. States didn't know what to do for them and had increasing numbers of seriously disturbed children; and there were reports from around the country of residential programs that had been torn apart and the staffs didn't know what to do. Facilities were actually empty and there were very few people in psychiatry or psychology that were interested in children. At that time I quite consciously decided that this is a problem the nation needs to work on.

Then I was invited to be on the First Joint Commission for Mental Illness and Health and again focused on children. I went to Europe and stayed there about three months for the joint commission and looked into programs for children in France, Scotland, and Italy and found a lot of fascinating work. France had a remarkable network of residential schools for all kinds of handicapped children—a program that was led by Robert Lafon, a psychiatrist at the University of Montpelier. He was professor of psychiatry and director of the Institute of Pedagogy at Montpelier, and president of the Association for Safeguard of Children. So, I learned a great deal from them, and the central idea was the idea of the "educateur," a young person usually, who was a full-time, reasonably well-trained child-care worker, but who was given responsibilities far transcending the kinds of responsibilities normally given to child-care workers in the United States. So, I got quite excited about that and recommended to the joint commission that there be some experimentation with this model.

I had seen us largely in the United States—and still do today—using very expensive and elaborately trained personnel for very brief periods of time with children and then leaving children to the care of marginal people for most of their daily lives. I became not only convinced that we ought to change it but indignant that we allowed it to continue.

So, we began to work on a concept of a program for children

that would utilize carefully selected, reasonably well trained, but not extensively trained people—following generally the "educateur" model but translated for use in this country. The joint commission endorsed the idea and then several colleagues of mine at Peabody and I drew up a plan for a project that would test the idea. And this was ultimately project Re-Ed— reeducation of emotionally disturbed children, one of the first large demonstration projects sponsored by NIMH.

To make a too long story short, we set up a training program at Peabody and two residential schools for disturbed kids —one at Nashville, one in Durham, the Nashville one connected with Peabody and Vanderbilt, the Durham one connected with Duke. We were just trying to learn how to work with children, using the personnel that we called teacher counselors and using psychiatrists and psychologists and pediatricians and educators in a very different role—as *consultants* to these young people—the young people carrying the full responsibility for the program.

It really has worked; those schools are still in existence; they survived the termination of the NIMH grant; the states picked up the costs, which is pretty unusual. They are residential schools but with a very strong emphasis on the ecological setting of the child and a great deal of work with the family and the neighborhood and the child's home. Well, the idea has caught on reasonably well. There are other schools around the country we know are definitely patterned after it—probably a dozen. The Skinnerian philosophy is not omitted, but we have just taken the view that the Skinnerian model is too simple for human beings.

It seems to me that some of the ideas of social scientists have had quite powerful impact. The program at Peabody has really done remarkably well in trying to anticipate the major national requirements regarding children. We began in Re-Ed; Susan Gray started what was then called "cultural deprivation" long before other people did. We had the first NIMH training program for research psychologists in mental retardation.

The Shrivers were interested in mental retardation and we had a strong program here, so they came down. We started the Kennedy Center at Peabody which is now a great and flourishing child-development research center. Shriver got to know Sue Gray during Peace Corps days and then when he went to the OEO he knew about her work. The staff study that was backup for starting OEO, the first article that was summarized by the staff, was Sue Gray's work, and Shriver subsequently made a public statement that it was Sue Gray's work that got him thinking in the direction of Head Start.

JAMES P. COMER *As a psychiatrist for children and families, Comer became aware of the extrapersonal as well as the interpersonal factors involved in the causation of emotional problems. When the patient or client was a member of a minority social group, the primary roles of these influences, particularly that of the school and the teachers, were apparent. Comer, believing in the possibilities of intervention and of prevention when noxious socioeconomic and psychological elements threaten the health of children, undertook a program in two ghetto schools in New Haven, with the aim of reducing the frequency and severity of the problems. In the following excerpt he discusses this experiment.*

We had a school program which was a joint effort between the Yale Child Study Center and the New Haven school system in which we were in two schools for five years and continued on in one of those schools for the past two years in which we tried to apply the principles of the behavioral sciences to all aspects of the school program, all the way from working with the problem child to working with the principal about the management of the school, procedures, and so on. We involved parents in critical decision-making activities and involved parents in a way that worked to support the school program—extracurricular activities and so on—and to bring the healthy aspects of the culture of the community into the school; the church choir was in the school, fashion shows [were] in the school—all in support of the school program. With that kind of contact and involvement in the critical institution affecting the lives of their children, we not only had improved academic performance of children but we also had parents mobilized. We had one parent who was simply not functioning well prior to the program that got involved and eventually became the head of the parent's group and is now back in college. We have other parents in the same situation who have now taken responsible jobs.

I think it was education and involvement which gave people a sense of value, importance, in a sense that they could make something happen. I think one of the critical problems in this society today is the feeling that you can't make anything happen. A kind of apathy has developed and when parents are affected then it affects children and it affects the institutions that work with children, and I think that's a very great problem.

6 Should Research on Children Be Geared to Social Relevance?

Research must aim to create the framework of action; in the life of the world there are things that need to be affirmed and things that need, above all, to be done.

August Heckscher, 1959 Annual Report,
The Twentieth Century Fund

SIBYLLE ESCALONA

I believe that better understanding of the human creature in the way it develops and functions is a worthwhile end in itself, quite independent of applications—immediate or delayed. I regret the enormous emphasis on immediate application that is not only imposed in a policy sort of way in relation to funds, but really has become a part of the thinking of very many people. I think that this is a retrogressive development and I think that one could trust what's been true in history all the time—that is, if phenomena in nature become more solidly and more accurately understood, these can be trusted to influence programs and actions and behaviors and social institutions. I reject the idea that we ought to put priority on the things for which we see immediate application, partly because I think that they of necessity are so circumscribed and delimited that the generalizations drawn from them and the applications made on their basis stand an awfully high chance of being unsuccessful. I also have the principal feeling that you do not need to say, "Well, if we understood this better, then you will be able to prevent cognitive retardation or any other evil." It doesn't seem to me to be a necessary reason. But I think ultimately the more we understand, the better we understand, the better we'll know what to do, as has been true with any other science or field of human endeavor even beyond science.

JEROME KAGAN

When I was younger I wanted to discover knowledge that would be of maximal utility to society. I did basic research, but the gap between data and utility is always enormous in psychology. Four years ago I began—and we're finishing the work this year—to work on my first applied problem. It is about as socially relevant a piece of research as one could implement in 1973. We are conducting an experiment to assess how day care influences infants. The population is working and middle class, Caucasians and Chinese, living in the South End of Boston. The infants enroll in the day-care center at three-and-a-half months and graduate at thirty months. They attend five days a week. And each child is yoked to a control child of the same ethnicity, social class, and sex who is being reared at home. We run the day-care center and can control the experience of the infants. Although I hope this study will be of value I must confess it isn't satisfying because this kind of field research is so noisy one is unsure of the knowledge. And lately my aesthetic needs in scientific work have become stronger. So I may initiate that class of research again. Although we will say something of social relevance which has some practicality, there is not enough beauty in the enterprise.

LESTER SONTAG *Lester Sontag began his medical career as a pediatrician who became interested and involved in research on child development. As originator and long-time director of the Fels Institute at Yellow Springs, Ohio, he stimulated and supported a variety of important research projects, aimed often at having clinical application for the benefit of children. His own interests increasingly centered on studies of infant and child behavior.*

I know of no instance where a research institute in practically any area has survived indefinitely without a strong research product which is of social or scientific value and which can be translated sooner or later, in part or in whole, into beneficial changes in the modes of operation, of handling, of creation of environment for human beings. Longitudinal research originally depended too much upon the detailed presentation of case records which included information in a variety of disciplines, and by a variety of observers, and was over a period of time. Unfortunately, a substantial devotion of effort to this area was unprofitable since, while it described the characteristics in the environment and the nutrition and the health of an individual, it did not produce communicable scientific knowledge, knowledge which sooner or later could be applied toward the production of better methods of nutrition, of creation of environment, of parent education, of motivating children, or of anything else. While it is of interest to read about an individual child, the limitations I think are obvious.

The problems in the area of human motivation, personality formation, education, etc., do not often lend themselves to the "brass instrument" approach. One must devise the research instruments and methods very different in form, and which are much more difficult to create, if they are to be sophisticated enough to yield the desired information.

Virginia Crandall's research, for example, illustrates this point of view very well. She is studying academic achievement motivation, a subject which in our time is of very primary importance, and which requires the very careful creation of methodology and instruments for its study. Yet the subject matter is so important that the effort to create the necessary instruments and methodology is fully justified. Crandall's works, with the instruments she has devised, have yielded information invaluable in the field of education. It is the kind of research product which justifies the high cost of support of the longitudinal method.

HAROLD STEVENSON *Harold Stevenson was trained as a psychologist. He has been a leader in child development, as a researcher, as a former director of the University of Minnesota Institute of Child Development and as an officer and active member of the Society for Research in Child Development. Frequently he has been a consultant to persons in and out of the federal government planning legislation for children's benefits. He is presently a professor of psychology in the Center For Human Growth and Development at the University of Michigan, Ann Arbor.*

I think there is a great disenchantment with the gathering of information that has no practical consequence. Once you introduce anything that has practical concern, the interest of very able students is very great. When you go off into the more esoteric, the interest of a large number of them begins to decline. So whether we like it or not, I think, whether the professor likes it or not, he is propelled into doing research, or considering things, that have practical consequences. I think we do have methodological sophistication, and I think people now are so much better trained. You combine those two things with this concern about the practical affairs of the child, and I think we're really going to make some progress.

WILLIAM KESSEN

Trends come and go with more speed than I can really track, but what seems to be happening at the moment is a commitment to problems of great consequence and relevance. Graduate students want to work with mothers; they want to see what the child is like out there—with a marvelous belief that the only way you can really do child-development research is to go and do a laboratory study. And seeing as how the faculty *doesn't* believe that, we have a marvelous task persuading the graduate students that the things they want to do are perfectly legitimate in the way of research. And I think that kind of change will take place with the kind of thing that a number of people are doing both here and elsewhere; the graduate students will realize that you can do hard-headed, analytical research in natural settings. And I think that is the direction we will be going in. The good laboratory studies of perception, the good laboratory studies of memory, the good laboratory studies of learning will not disappear, but they will be enlarged by this field kind of research.

I want to mention, as one last parting emphasis, the vital importance of researchers being in touch with the phenomena—I have to be very careful with this because I don't want to reduce my commitment to formal experimental procedures—as a way of getting ideas, of keeping in touch, of seeing what the display of phenomena is like, of avoiding the belief that one little piece of the field represents the entire thing. However important it is, it isn't the whole thing. I think it's terribly important for graduate students and senior researchers themselves to be in a clinical setting or be in a school, or have some social responsibility, or be involved in government circles either at the local or federal level, just to keep some sense of what the problems are.

SHELDON WHITE

You take a kid who comes in as an undergraduate and he wants to know something about human nature, he very often wants to help people, and he comes in with sort of big questions about life, and you grind him fine, you teach him to be a scientist. So you begin with arenas of concern, then you are taught an art form and then you spend the rest of your life trying to get back to doing something interesting. OK, that in a nutshell, I think, is the issue, the central issue for anyone who works in the field.

I teach a course here [Harvard] called "Child Development and Social Policy." In a number of ways I am trying to, sort of, get the graduate students who come past me a little bit more ready to answer the kinds of questions that can come from the outside. I am trying to get them to see right at the beginning that there is such a thing as society. I am trying to get them to see right at the beginning that there is a social frame. Yes, and in their research too.

When I came here as an undergraduate they told me, "Look, kid, those big questions are nice but here are the ones you can do research on." They told me, basically, "You can't work on that problem. You can't ask a clean question, therefore you can't get a scientific answer. The most important thing is to get a scientific answer, and then we will get back to those questions—but stick with this stuff." And, I think, implicitly they said, "That's where the money was, and that's where the status was, and that's how you passed this course," and so forth. They certainly said all that. Well, I don't think they had to do that; they could have told me, "Look, your question is a good question, it's not a bad question; in fact, it's the right question."

I try very hard now, with undergraduates, not to tell them that they have got bad questions. You have to, basically, teach them how to love the issues as well as how to love the data. And I guess I might say, you try a little bit, you can't do everything. You try a little bit with the next generation not to force this kind of extreme that I went through, to try to develop the coexistence of both the issues and the questions.

WALTER MONDALE

Some of the studies get awful esoteric but I don't want to criticize that because maybe someday somebody will come up with something. I believe scientists have to go where their minds ask them to go. I don't think politicians can start demanding. I think that is one of the troubles with science today; we have been pounding the scientific community too hard for result-oriented, immediate returns, and some of the pure research has suffered.

LEON EISENBERG

I see a major role for the child-development psychologists, but only if they move out of the university setting and schools for children of graduate students and professors. You can just do so much in studying the paths of development you see under these precious and artificially arranged circumstances. I think they need to be out in the slums, they need to be in the school system, they need to be in daily life; they have the methods, they have the tradition; if they are interested in attacking real social problems, I think they can make an important contribution. The dilemma is, of course, as always, that the more important the problem, the sloppier it tends to be and the more difficult it is to be a "scholar." Well, I think you can pick something in between the precision of elegant answers to trivial questions and imprecise answers to important ones and sacrifice elegance in the hope of greater relevance when it comes to child development.

I must—I can't pass the opportunity by—say that a hell of a lot of current child-development research is research in trivia. I remember a paper published with the sponsorship of some research grant, in which a small number of children were studied for the impact of giving allowances to children of different ages in different amounts. I couldn't have cared less; no important question had been asked; no important data had been accumulated. This is one of the real flaws of the literature—and you just have to look through a fine journal like *Child Development*—and I would say two-thirds of what is in it could be omitted without any substantial loss to the knowledge base.

My argument is not relevance because God knows any physician recognizes how remote from practicality the most important studies have seemed to be at the beginning. It isn't because it doesn't have immediate applicability, it's that it's being done for no other reason than to get a master's or doctor's degree and get the hell out of the university. Or your professor sponsors it because if you do a small problem suitable for available methods he gets another publication for his bibliography. It's make-work; it's trivia. These folks are bright enough; they are just as moral as anyone else, and I don't mean to degrade them. Why the hell don't they get out of the university nursery school and go to work in a slum school right outside the university where kids aren't learning? If we can apply academic methods to real-life problems, I think we will get much better theses, and the research investment will yield much more substantial knowledge. Developmental psychologists ought to be working in the pediatric clinics, they ought to be in the psychiatric hospitals. They have much to teach us. I mean in no way to degrade them, but what they are is precious and what we are is clumsy. Somewhere in between is the scholar with the social conscience to apply his skills to disadvantaged children.

7 What Are the Priorities in the Battle to Improve the Lives of Children?

There seems to be a folk tradition around this town that it's somehow indecent to cut any social program. I don't think the second administration will be a believer in that folk tale. I think a President with a substantial mandate, who feels the majority of the people are behind him, will feel very comfortable in saying to a vested interest group, such as the social workers, "Look, your social program of the 1960's isn't working, and we're going to dismantle it so you'll just have to go out and find honest labor somewhere else."

John D. Ehrlichman

The sporadic and piecemeal way in which programs for children have been organized in this country has resulted in a rabbit warren of overlapping, inadequately funded, poorly supervised programs, scattered about in various agencies of government. Many of them have been badly designed in terms of child welfare because other concerns of society had a large influence in their planning. For example, the great day-care effort of World War II was mounted to free mothers to work in the factories; Head Start was rushed into being at least in part because it was perceived as a viable undertaking for the community-action programs called for in the Economic Opportunity Act of 1964; the vetoed Child Development Act of 1971, which called for massive federal expenditures for various types of developmental day-care programs for children of every economic class (the bill has been compared to Medicare in its magnitude), had backers who had many interests besides the healthy development of young children. The women's liberation movement saw the legislation as providing the means to get women out of the home; minority groups looked upon it as a way to get power into the hands of the community and parents' organizations, others liked it primarily because it would free mothers on relief to earn their own living, and so it went.

Edward Zigler, the former head of the Office of Child Development, discussed the problems of getting good programs for children in his interview with me. He said that people are not willing to abandon their own self-interest, or the interest of their particular political or philosophical position, and give up something in doing something in behalf of children. He remembered going around Washington before the Child Development Act was vetoed begging people to give in a little to the point of view of others in order to wind up with something that would help children. But, he said, "to some people the important thing in that bill was that we hire poor people, for others it was that parents have control of the center. For others it was this, for others it was that. One doesn't really get a sense that people ever start the other way around and say, 'Look, here's a child and his family. What does one mount that will optimally meet their needs?' Of course, whatever position one takes on this they always justify and rationalize that that's what they are talking about. But I never really get a sense of that's where it is."

If we are ever to provide properly for the nation's children and straighten out the chaos of the existing programs, it will be because the American people wish to do so. Only the insistence of the voters can combat the entrenched interests and ideological prejudices which impede progress in this direction. But first the voters must be informed of the present situation and select priorities for action. My discussions on the subject of what children need the most *now* were initiated in the hopes of helping in this process.

JUSTINE WISE POLIER *Justine Polier is a distinguished jurist, recently retired from a long career as a judge on the Family and Children's Court of New York City. She is now a member of the staff of the Children's Defense Fund. There, as director of the Juvenile Justice Division, she works for greater justice before the law, especially for children of minority groups who get into trouble, and too frequently are incarcerated in institutions without due process and without any effort made to rehabilitate them.*

The following statement was made in a personal letter to me.

If I were to rank first priorities of needs of children in the U.S., I would put recognition that the fact of birth should entitle a child to the protection and benefits from government that would assure decent support, health care, and education necessary for healthy development. At the present time approximately 8 million children are forced to survive below the poverty line. We have not developed a system for delivery of health services to children. Their medical and psychological problems are not identified or met in a vast proportion of cases. They are forced to grow up in unhealthy housing and they are not provided with education to evoke their true potential. The failures of society hit hardest at poor children of whom a disproportionate number are nonwhite. I believe that unequal protection and discriminatory requirements imposed on children or their parents by reason of poverty should be treated as a suspect classification in violation of their constitutional rights.

NICHOLAS HOBBS

I would put the money on trying to do what we can to make the normal socializing agencies work. I would not put it into individual psychotherapy or into individual treatments; you do that as a humane kind of thing but you can't solve the problem that way. I'd say we have either got to make the American family work . . . and make it a stable way to build a society, or we have got to invent a substitute for it. We cannot survive the way we are doing now. We've got to make neighborhoods places for nurturance of children, and we've got to make public schools—down to age zero—especially for handicapped kids that have an impediment for life—effective in their role.

ALBERT QUIE

Congressman Albert Quie is the ranking Republican on the House Education and Labor Committee. He has played a major role in shaping education legislation in the Congress. He was interviewed so that his views might be juxtaposed with those of his fellow Minnesotan Walter Mondale. Both men share a concern for children in trouble and a feeling that guidance is needed from researchers in child development to foster legislation for children that will be effective, nonharmful, and economically feasible. Although they are members of opposing political parties, Congressman Quie and Vice President Mondale exchanged research information on this issue freely. Quie was instrumental in the enactment of legislation guaranteeing public education programs to all handicapped children.

... There is not an adequate research effort. Secondly, we have not put together an adequate program of dissemination, and I would like to see a move in dissemination of the research information in a way we did in agriculture. You can't have the educational so-called agent a person who is totally financed by the federal government because it would be viewed as a higher level of government trying to impose its will. The genius of the county agent in agriculture was that the local people paid for a portion of that salary and secondly, that that person was tied to the research institution, a land-grant college, and so it brought together research and the farmer in a way that both would accept. And then, I believe the teacher-training institutions ought to be more closely tied with the elementary and secondary schools and the preschool programs so that the changes that are needed to meet the needs of children can be brought to the attention of the teacher-training institution early. It seems to me the teacher-training institutions have often been fifteen to twenty years behind the times so that our necessity now is really for upgrading and retraining the teachers out there in the field. That, I think, has the top priority, and once that is brought to bear, then the need for improvement will be felt in the local communities and they will utilize their resources to accomplish it.

MARGARET MEAD *This renowned anthropologist, recently retired from the staff of the American Museum of Natural History, has had a lifetime interest in families, their structure and function. Her views were sought on the changing American family and the significance of these changes for our children.*

I think the present extreme communes, hippie communes, are a very temporary sort of symptom, but I think that we're going to move away from the isolated nuclear family which is the worst possible place to bring up a child. I wrote the first article on this subject in something like 1927 after I had been to Samoa where I saw the tremendous advantages for children to be brought up with a large number of relatives. I've been interested in this all the way along—the consequences of the two-generation family, the isolation from grandparents, the isolation from any picture of what age is going to be like, the fragility of the family, the absence of models of other kinds of people so that if a boy has his mother's mind he has great difficulty interpreting who he is in terms of identity; if you have a few more people around a boy may find other men with the same kind of mind or kind of interest he has.

What I'm talking about at present is the need for a kind of town planning which will assure clusters of people living together of different ages; they don't need to be biologically related. It would be a place where young people who aren't married can live, where unmarried people can live, and widows can live, related to a series of small families around which they can cluster and provide models for the children, taking care of the children, taking the weight off the young couples. Under present conditions children need so much more adult time per child than they used to need on the farms.

SHELDON WHITE

I think the problem is not to give the kids more vitamins so that they can go to school; the problem is not to put out another group of professionals who would coordinate the first group of professionals. We have to look at housing, and we have to look at social ecology. We have to look at the designs, designs for a system in which child-rearing is possible. I have argued for several years, but I can't get HUD and OCD to sit down together and start doing some planning. I'd try to get a little bit outside of cost-benefit calculations, and market calculations and I would start trying to ask, "What are the best arrangements of the social contracts and of the housing arrangements so that families and kids can grow up?"

Through the miracle of modern statistics, we can now predict at age three who is not going to be employed when he is eighteen. If he is black, if his IQ is low, if he has any kind of major handicap, if he is an Indian kid, if he is a rural kid, if the parents have low education, we can correlationally estimate that he has a low probability of getting a job; therefore, we call him "disadvantaged," and we proceed to try to fix his childhood. That part of the problem lies in the design of our society, which provides in fact restricted opportunities for people to play a productive part in the economy. I was saying to somebody one day, "What we need is not income redistribution; we need work distribution."

ROBERT ALDRICH

I found I had to learn what the structure and functions of cities are because this is where the children live; and a growing, developing child is very much influenced by the nature of the surroundings in which he grows and develops. In other words, the city is a part of the child's growth and development and I suspect we could document that cities can make children sick and that they can also inhibit to some extent sick children from getting well as fast as they might. I have pretty good evidence for this. So then this became another major project in my career and interest. I've developed a small group of people working with architects and engineers and urban planners who are trying to learn how to apply the principles of growth and development, physical, social, and behavioral, to the process of planning cities.

How do you plan cities that make it possible for children and youth to have a really good experience of growth and development? There are dozens and dozens of simple little questions that I guess have never been asked in the process of designing a city. One of my favorites is the whole street-crossing problem. How fast does it take a three-year-old to walk across a street intersection compared with a thirty-year-old athletic male? This has to do with timing of stoplights, and whether you permit right turns and a lot of other things. By asking some very specific questions of these architects and engineers we set up a dialogue which really was first developed in Athens where the biological, medical types and the social-science types, sitting on one side of the table and talking with the architects and engineers on the other, would begin to agree that if we were going to make a city for man or a city for people or a city for children you've really got to have some scientific evidence, some scientific data. It's not a question of opinion anymore, it's a matter of getting researchable questions out on the table and getting evidence to answer them. This to me is one of the most enormous unresearched areas, brand-new virgin territory that I know of—namely, what are the questions in city design and city function that can be answered from growth and development that will make these cities livable for man during different parts of his life cycle. This is what I think pediatricians should do. I think this is one of the big areas for the application of our knowledge of child health.

URIE BRONFENBRENNER

In my recent work it's become clear to me that one of the major institutions determining the welfare of the children in the United States is business and industry . . . through the way in which it determines what families do or do not do. One of the major recommendations that I've been pushing via the 1970 White House Conference on Children, in which I had a very arduous responsibility, is the notion of a free part-time employment practices act which would make it illegal to discriminate against someone—a parent—who wants to work part-time because he's a family person. And notice I say "parent," not mother.

I want it to be clear that what is involved here is not just working on legislation. That's a very important thing, but essentially, as I see it, an understanding of human development is going to require us to become concerned with all the major institutions of our society, many of which have not been recognized as having an impact on children at all. Take transportation. Public transportation is tremendously important because it's a far different world when you have public transportation and ride on a train or in a bus with kids than when you have to drive a car, or continue to have public transportation . . . as it is—age-segregated so that school buses have only children in them. I don't want to imply that technology necessarily dehumanizes. I don't think so at all. Technology is what we make it. You could use technology to make a more human society if you choose.

What we need to do is to reinvent the wheel, that is to re-create now as social technologists situations which used to happen inevitably when you had no artificial mobility and artificial communication, and you had to deal face to face with human beings, and you stayed in the same place for a long period of time. Now we have to rediscover that it's important to stay in the same place for a longer period of time, that it's important to walk and to talk, rather than to go at sixty or seventy miles an hour, because when you're going sixty or seventy miles an hour you can't have an emotional scene, and emotional scenes are important. That's how human beings are made. Of course, television becomes very important here. As I've said, television is important, not for the behavior it produces (I'm not half as worried about this aggression bit that we're all wound up about) as the behavior it prevents because when the television set is on the father and the mother and the son can't have their arguments and scenes and damns and the whole rest of it. You put the whole process of socialization and mutual socialization in formaldehyde while this thing is on.

I think probably that child advocacy may not have a long life. Maybe I'm engaging in some wishful thinking here, but I think that in perspective I now see a great weakness in an orientation with which I was very strongly identified, namely, the child-centered approach. And advocacy is still a child-centered approach. We have to become family-centered, community-centered, neighborhood-centered, because there is no way of facilitating the development of the child except through the systems in which he has to grow. It's like saying, "I'm going to be a plant-centered corn-grower." You can't be a plant-centered corn-grower. You've got to look at the earth, the water, and the fertilizer, and the whole bit. I think one of the reasons why we've missed the mark is we've thought that a person working with an individual child could somehow accomplish the necessary job.

More and more I have become impressed as I look at the data in the field that people become what the institutions allow them or encourage them to become. And the whole magic of the American dream (which is a nightmare at the moment but I don't believe is dead) is that we have as this fundamental premise the notion of pluralism—that there is no single theory that's right. We are pragmatists. We're willing to try and if something doesn't work we give it up. We don't say that because it's holy we have to keep it up. And therefore, I see some hope even in this period of obviously great disorganization.

ELIZABETH WICKENDEN

The whole question of the relationship of the child to the family to the larger community is really central to this whole problem. We have seen one thing that could certainly make us feel hopeful; we have seen over the course of the last two hundred years a complete change of attitude toward education. Whereas it was originally assumed that the family was responsible for the education of a child and either paid for it or did it at home or it didn't occur, we did see in New York City a sense of entitlement for education all the way through college as a community obligation toward all children. And in all states we have seen the growth of the idea that every child is entitled to a public education through high school. And so, taking that as a precedent, one might be hopeful that some of the other areas like child health, child welfare, and child development would likewise come to be seen as a concern of the total community.

I think the most shocking thing that President Nixon did was to write in his veto of the Child Development bill that this was a direct attack and threat to the American family. If you think that any form of community support for children is threatening to the family, naturally people will tend to recoil. Therefore, we need a philosophical base in which we see an interaction of the child with his family into the larger community, with no one part of the encircling environment being threatening to another.

KENNETH KENISTON

I am critical of the exclusive emphasis we have given to reforming the individual and targeting programs at parents only. It seems to me that throughout our history we have tended to say parents are to blame, and we have often imposed a kind of middle-class and moralistic standard upon poor people, or nonwhite people, or people in difficulties, which has stigmatized those people and made them feel worse. However well intentioned, we have really failed to look at the whole society and [ask] why we constantly regenerate a lower class . . . and what we could do about the largely economic factors and social factors that regenerate that class with that group of children. That would be the number one problem.

We ought to be thinking how families—how parenting—can be supported, and not how families can be replaced and not about what we can do to provide alternatives for the family. We ought to be thinking—in the long term—about work arrangements for mothers and fathers that would make it possible for them to parent their children without enormous sacrifices of career and livelihood. We ought to be thinking about that kind of out-of-family child care which supports the family and not that which replaces it. So we ought to be thinking about very small units, for example, that are controlled by parents and not about enormous centers. We ought to be thinking about neighborhoods.

We often mystify the nature of the problem. What's wrong is not bad parents or disturbed children, but the context, the ecology, in Bronfenbrenner's term, in which both parents and children grow up which severely limits what they can and cannot do. If we only concentrate on Head Start programs or even individual therapy, without also looking at what's going on in the rest of the child's life or the parents' life—the nature of their work, the quality of the community they live in, the availability of personal and professional supports, their income, the way in which the society treats their skin color, the job openings that are available, the general quality of life, the morale of the places they live in—we can reform individuals and educate small children until we are blue in the face and exhaust all our national resources. I suspect it will save some people, a few individuals can be helped, but the problems will simply perpetuate themselves.

I think Gilbert Steiner has said this—it has often been the case that those people concerned with children and families in this country have been very generous but they also have been rather moralistic and in a way their goals have been goals of moral uplift, which is very hard for public policy to respond to in a good way. You cannot legislate virtue although you can legislate income redistribution. One of the things that it is important to acknowledge is that public agencies and governments may be able to create a context within which children grow up as vital and as committed and as caring human beings, but it can in no way guarantee the creation of vital, moral, and caring people.

JAMES P. COMER

I think that child-care people emphasized, or overemphasized, the whole business of intellectual development in the sixties and seventies in a way that we paid very little attention to the social and moral development and that was harmful. I think we have to stress now the importance of social and moral development and show the relatedness between government and institutions and certain kinds of strengths and problems in families and children. I think that's where you start. But it's not only talking about it and writing about it. I think there's going to have to be enough model programs and structured arrangements where people can begin to understand very directly that there's a relationship between ignoring certain children and certain problems. We're already to the point that even many middle-income children are beginning to reflect some of the consequences of our failure with children over the past.

One of the biggest problems, I think, that exists in this country is the failure to build new towns in the forties rather than suburban sprawls. I think that's unrelated to children directly . . . but if we had had many, many, new towns around our large cities we would have avoided much of the isolation, the alienation. We could have had communities of the size that would have provided security, contact between people of different groups. That decision has had a direct effect on children, the quality of life, the quality of the developmental experience. Even now, I know that HEW and HUD hardly talk to each other, and yet the decisions being made are very important in relation to education and welfare.

MARIAN WRIGHT EDELMAN

The Comprehensive Child Development bill of 1971 is basically still, I think, sound. I think that what it said in terms of what the nation's commitment to children should be was important and I don't think we should hedge on it. It said you ought to have comprehensive services and what we meant by comprehensive was our model in Head Start, including health services, nutrition services, educational services of some undefined kind, but some educational help, and whatever else kind of help that family needed. And that means, I think, helping a family to deal with welfare, helping a family to get the kind of advocacy it needs to provide adequately for that child. Secondly, the bill stated that priority should go to poor children and children of single-parent families, but that it should not be a poor people's program. And we wrote an allocation which was an attempt to redefine "poor" to hit the working middle-class folk . . . and to say a third should go to the middle-class women. We don't want any more poor people's programs. The third thing was that we thought there should be some adequate parental involvement. What we know is that intervention programs work best with parents and that's something we're not willing to concede on. The last thing was that there should be a substantial financial commitment at the federal level. I'm tired of always having the debates about . . . choosing between school lunch and school milk programs, or choosing between child development and welfare and a decent income maintenance. And I just think we've got to begin, slow as that's going to be, changing the terms of debate about what it is we've got to choose from to help children in this country. I think we can afford to spend . . . 10 billion dollars a year on child-development programs. And I think it's not an either/or income-maintenance system. We're still going to need services even if we do have adequate wages.

The amazing thing to me is not so much Mr. Nixon's veto (which I still have not gotten over quite because I didn't believe he'd do it and that shows my residual naiveté) but that you could put together a bill of this kind and get it through the Congress in less than a year. We lost; we almost won, which was fantastic. But we lost and folks said, "You can't do it." I mean, that's just ridiculous. You go back year after year until you get it. It's going to be harder to get it now; there's going to be more debate. But it seems to me if you're committed to a thing you go back. The children still have needs.

Any old legislation is not going to be good enough for kids, and I think the worst thing we could do would be to get too involved in the political process to the point where we get major federal commitments for something that's not going to be healthy in the long run. I consider minimum in any bill, very basic policy control for parents. I consider minimum some kind of socioeconomic mix in terms of eligibility criteria so that you're not just repeating the lessons of Head Start. I think you won't have all the social-science evaluations going on in all these crazy ways if it's not just poor kids being talked about. I consider minimum that you have enough of a federal commitment in money terms where you won't be doing less than what you've got. I mean if you get *so* little money you're going to end up with custodial care, I'm afraid, or you're going to run up against very real fairness questions in terms of which kids you serve and which not. I think the comprehensive developmental thing is still important . . . like health care, like nutrition, like some kind of educational component, like advocacy—a commitment in those centers to helping families become more independent, to helping families deal with their children better.

LOIS MEEK STOLZ

Having participated in the FERA nursery schools of the Depression, in the war nurseries during World War II, and even later now in the Head Start program, I feel like saying I'm sick and tired of the government's stopgap programs for young children. These programs are always brought about by some social calamity. They're not brought about by thinking through what is important for children on a long-range basis. I think it's really high time that the government put funds into having a *continuous* program for children from birth up to school age, and that this should be planned in terms of consultation centers and clinics for babies, and nursery schools and consultation for the preschool years. . . . These are the formative years. We know all about it now; we know how much socialization affects it, and we do nothing but stir up a lot of dust that doesn't stand. We take untrained people because we can't find trained ones, and here at the end of my life I'm getting tired of it.

MARTHA PHILLIPS *Martha Phillips is presently a member of the House Ways and Means Committee staff. When interviewed she was director of the research committee for the Republican members of the*

U.S. House of Representatives. She admitted that her concern about day care arose from her experiences as a working mother of a preschool aged child, and that this influenced her decision to encourage members of her political party in the Congress to endorse legislation in the field of child care and development.

I'll tell you one thing that I realize. I don't know how many Congressmen realize it, but I feel it very strongly. There's no program that you can inflict on a child, or magic pill, or inoculation, or anything like that, that you can give to a child for a six-month period or a one-year period . . . at a certain age, that will ensure that that kid's going to turn out okay and grow up and at age twenty five or thirty be a responsible, contributing member of society. Any parent knows that kids will not pick up their room or wash behind their ears unless every day you say, "Pick up your room and wash behind your ears." Every day. The first day that you don't say it, that's when the ears go dirty. I think with child-development programs and any child programs that it's the same thing, that you have to keep doing it. It's only good as long as you're doing it and when you stop, things start disintegrating. This certainly was the experience, I think, with Head Start. They tried taking kids for six weeks in the summer, giving them a razzmatazz program, and some injections, and a little feeding, and then expected to go back five years later and find that these children had IQs that were twenty points higher than the ones who hadn't been subjected to this. What could be more patently ridiculous? You know, if they had kept children in an enriched program during those five years, then you'd find at the end of five years that just the fact that somebody extra was caring for them and doing for them and making them feel important probably would have had some sort of measurable effect. But there's no way you can do a quick and easy job. Somebody's got to put in the time, the effort, the hours. And that's very expensive.

I'm not convinced that you need to have day-care centers because if you look at what the country can afford, even pretend we didn't have any national defense, how much do you want to pay out of your taxes or out of your salary to buy care? And what is the best way to spend it? Obviously the cheapest thing is for kids to stay home with their mothers because that's a different kind of a subsidy and it's not a monetary subsidy except indirectly. But in terms of what you can pay for, maybe for many children—and I found this to be the case for my own child out of all the options (and we tried quite a few)—the very, very best thing for her was to go into somebody else's home who also had children, who had some of the same sort of mothering and discipline and hand-washing kinds of philosophies that I had and would take care of my child as if it were her own.

I'm in favor of high-quality family day care (and God help the person who has to enforce it or inspect it or try to bring it about)—the combination of that plus teaching people better how to take care of their own children plus, I think, some sort of cognitive development inputs that you can provide . . . maybe some sort of a nursery-school approach in the morning for the older children and your health inputs, your nutrition inputs. But why does a day-care center with 120 kids divided up in 1 : 5 teacher/child ratios have to be the magic answer? It's very much more difficult to bring about coordinated, warm, responsive family day care or babysitters or homemakers.

PETER SAUER *Although Peter Sauer is a marine biologist by training, his career now involves a variety of duties under the rubric of "community organizer and consultant on day care."*

He has little patience with the cloistered researcher and his esoteric studies, however scientific they may be. At the Bank Street College of Education he works with a team of professionals, parents, and generalists who are impatient with traditional approaches in child care and education and who prefer working in the field (that is, the community) "where the action is," especially when it involves them in intensely personal relationships with poor people.

I have been trying to understand . . . what are the reasons that the concept of working with families has been so distorted and confused by professionals. They don't say this but they feed into the general national misconception that if we have a lot of good day-care programs somehow or other a lot of people will have to be less parents, somehow or other day care can supplement parenting. And the other confusion is that parent participation is always described in terms of bringing in the parent and never other adults or siblings engaged in child rearing; uncles and aunts are not counted.

There are several principles involved in changing things. The first one is to understand that parents and other family childrearers are predominant in child rearing and in any helping system, whether it's health, or recreation, or education, or child care. Child care services that don't recognize and support families will not only wind up *not* helping the parents but will fragment the family structure, pulling the people apart, making them dependent on outside experts. We have got to develop new ways of reaching the people who are already caring for kids and help them improve what they are doing. I mean parents primarily, but also there is that underground child-care network that is not half as bad as people think. There are plenty of studies going on . . . that discover that there is really something good in this family day-care business that people have been putting down for years. Right now, we are sort of stuck into stereotypes. When groups who are operating fairly good child-care programs go out looking for funds, whether from foundations or the government, they are forced to describe themselves in terms of stereotypical models, like a school. Why we assume that a child whose mother must go out to work . . . should then be put in a school, I can't imagine. Around the country there are groups of people doing direct consulting, direct information and referral about child-rearing. The entrance point is generally, "I need a babysitter," but the information that goes with that process is enormous—directly to the parents. Those organizations are helping people who want to care for children be in touch with those who need care for children, and there are ways of helping people who care for children do it better and of helping parents exercise more informed decisions. But those information-referral systems are not even considered to be child-care programs.

I think that if the Mondale bill were passed tomorrow we would have a day-care system roughly equivalent to nursing homes—large masses of money all controlled by a single Office of Child Development, extremely vulnerable to corruption and political agendas. The day-care centers in New York were in fact developed by a local system very similar to what that bill proposes, and 250 were built by a process that has nothing to do with children, that became totally involved in providing rent, enormous rents, over a long period of time. The community groups who finally got in there to control the programs had no opportunity to learn what they were doing and consequently in day-care centers that are entirely funded by the city, licensed by the Department of Health, staffed by professionals and people absolutely qualified, children are in fact raped; preschoolers have been raped in Brooklyn and in Manhattan in one center they were regularly stored in trash cans. That's the kind of system we are liable to get across the nation if we fall into the trap of thinking that one major government pot of money, one major government source of definition of who you are, is going to be the solution. I think it is really important to bring to everybody's attention—the press, people down the street, people you work with—the groups who are running different kinds of programs for children, programs which represent a more humanistic, less fantastically expensive approach.

It's pretty well documented that almost any community in the country has more people who want to care for children than there are children who need the care, so consequently, it's really a buyer's market. But one of the ways that bad day-care winds up exploiting parents and driving them absolutely bananas is that licensing has created a situation in which they are prevented from knowing that they have alternatives. In most communities there is not even a place where they can go to find out what a Head Start center is. When parents can make choices with information, parents are empowered to make more systematic the services they receive and the care their children receive.

MARIAN RADKE-YARROW *Marian Radke-Yarrow is a psychologist, chief of the Laboratory of Developmental Psychiatry, National Institute of Mental Health. Early in 1973 she traveled in mainland China as a member of a scientific study group interested in methods of child care, health care and education.*

Again, I suppose, I am drawing on some of my ideas from my experiences in China. Here in NIMH we talk along many times about problems of health-delivery services. We specialize everybody, you know. We specialize all the medical people and so on. Well, China, in my current kind of idealistic view of it, has produced an abundance of paraprofessionals which makes it possible for a family, a child, for any kind of problem to have contact with someone who can help. This can be a retired worker—they can be teachers, they can be chairman of a committee, and so on. I think we need paraprofessionals spread out in the schools, spread out in the churches, or wherever, that are available to children.

EDWARD ZIGLER

I think that the greatest need the nation has today is for child-care workers. The demand for them from the thousands of day-care centers that we already have, from the many more that we're planning for the future, from our Head Start centers —these manpower needs have never been met. I think it's because we haven't thought in large enough terms, nor in active, correct terms, in respect to economic viability and what makes for a good child-care worker.

There have been two paths that the nation has gone down in

this respect. One, pre-Head Start, was, of course, our typical B.A. early-childhood worker who tends to be quite well trained, quite adequate with the job at hand. However, what nobody realizes is that every extrapolation we do of people trained in that conventional route shows that it would be totally inadequate; it's inadequate now to man the Head Start centers and the day-care centers that we have, no less the explosion in these centers that we're expecting over the next few years. Another method we saw with Head Start was one in which a kind of naive romanticism captured the nation. We felt, "Well, gee, if you could just get a poor person and bring her into a Head Start center, she would be an ideal caretaker for the young." Well, we discovered that that isn't so. In a survey that we've done at Head Start centers where this philosophy did capture hiring practices for many years, we discovered that the vast majority of individuals caring for young children in Head Start (which ought to be, you know, the model program for the country) are not acquainted with the simplest principles of child development.

So, I say that the professional approach with a B.A. is not going to get the job done for us. And this notion that, "Gee, anyone can take care of a child—you just sweep up people who have some sense of co-feeling with children"—is simply not the way to surround children with those caretakers which will eventuate in the optimum development of children. What is left for this country then? I think what is left is the development of a brand-new institution, which other nations have managed to come up with but America has never managed—that is, we're calling it now, the child-development associate. This will be a person who's not as well-trained as our B.A. person, and will be a person who is trained in a different way. The emphasis will be not on the vast training that goes into a B.A.—the English literature, evolution, and biology, all of which is worthwhile to make a whole human being and perhaps a good teacher. But rather what we want to do with a CDA is to have circumscribed training directed at performance competency so that this person is not accredited on the basis of having spent so many hours in a classroom, but rather on the basis of being judged competent in performing very circumscribed things with children.

A day-care course is probably the largest need in the nation today. The percentage of working mothers is now 45 percent or so. Somebody has got to be concerned. I mean people are getting all hung up on the value issue: should mothers take care of their own children? Should children be in centers and so forth? I think arguing the value issue is naive. Mothers have already made that decision. Either for fiscal reasons they have to work or because of self-actualization reasons women work. So the next question is, how is society going to meet the new social condition which prevails, namely, working mothers and children in need of day care? Now, good day care is going to be the issue. That we're going to get more and more day care, you know, that's dictated by the number of working mothers. The problem is that so much of day care in this country is of such poor quality. In fact, some of it is clearly of the nature that is detrimental to the growth and development of children. I think of Mary Keyserling's recent book, *Windows on Day Care,* in which she documents these instances of children being tied to chairs, children being taken care of by people who are too ill or senile to care for children. These kinds of instances cannot be tolerated.

Well, the issue is not whether we're going to have more day care in this country, but rather what quality is it going to be? If day-care centers are going to supplement family life, then they've got to really do it. They've got to be concerned with the total development of the child, his health, his cognitive development, his personal and social development. They cannot simply be custodial warehouses where a child sits and watches TV for a couple of hours, and rides around on a tricycle in the backyard and that's it. They've really got to be growing places.

JULIUS RICHMOND

We're moving into a new era in which I would hope we would focus our attention much more on services for the universe of children within our communities rather than exclusively on parents or children who ultimately find their way to services. I have the conviction that if we apply the knowledge that we have now in the service of prevention of disease and also in the development of a healthy personality, as the 1950 White House Conference phrased it, that we can have a very favorable effect—by which I mean decreased need for various remedial and correctional services later on.

I think that if we could design a system where families are not lost to our various human services from the time of birth until the time children enter school we could minimize the developmental attrition. I think that through a program of continuity of care, applying the knowledge of child development that we have to all children in our communities, we might minimize not only developmental attrition but possibly such occurrences as child abuse and a group of related disorders that we have come to think about as social illnesses. I'm thinking of lead poisoning, failure to thrive through lack of stimulation, repetitive accidents, disorders of this nature, and possibly even some of the major psychiatric disorders that develop. One could also wonder whether increased attention to the child's development in the preschool period might not minimize the development of many of the so-called learning disorders which we deal with as children grow older.

What I am saying, in effect, is that we know where children are when they are born in this country because, with rare exceptions, they are registered; we know, by and large, where they are when they reach school age because legally they must register; but in between it's entirely a hit-or-miss proposition dependent almost exclusively upon the education of the parents, their motivation, and also upon the availability of resources to them. I think we are on the threshold of being able now to provide these services if we somehow or other can redistribute our manpower in more meaningful ways.

At the turn of the century we had individual, charismatic advocates for children and families who went out into the communities and were the movers and the shakers and the doers in an effort to apply the knowledge that we had. I think that with the increasing complexity of our country we now have to institutionalize our advocacy; there need to be groups of citizens with concerns about children who in one way or another will see that they don't get lost to services and who in a democratic society will maintain a pluralistic approach to the delivery of the varieties of services that children and families need, but not use pluralism as a defense against doing nothing or use it as an excuse for letting children fall between the cracks of services.

BENJAMIN SPOCK

I would say most basically that one of the first steps we should take is to eliminate poverty in the United States. I used to assume that a certain amount of poverty is inevitable in any society, but having gone through certain political experiences in the past ten years, which opened my eyes, I now realize that the Scandinavian countries, for example, long ago abolished their poverty and if they could do it we could afford to do it much more easily than they. I think rather than punitive laws, penalizing parents for such things as abuse of children, we've got to recognize that this is a fault of the whole society, and that we should pass laws giving economic security, giving housing, giving good medical care, giving good education to all our people.

TRUDE LASH *Her many years as executive director of the Citizen's Committee on Children of New York City provided Trude Lash with a knowledge of the "state of the child" in that city that few possess. Her experience has made her an exceptionally competent staff member in the Foundation for Child Development.*

I still am convinced that you have to make a minimum income available to everybody and that you can't have it below the poverty level. That's why I'm for a family allowance. That, I think, is most important. And, you know when we established the goals for this new National Council of Organizations I, among a small group, insisted that as part of our goals we have first to work for decent incomes. I was involved in the 1962 Ribicoff committee which suggested amendments to the Social Security laws, and I no longer believe we were right. Then we said if you provide services for people *before* they become welfare clients, you can prevent dependence. I don't believe that any more. *First* you have to have *money* for a decent way of life.

ABRAHAM BERGMAN *This physician effectively combines clinical work and teaching, holding positions both as director of outpatient services of the Children's Orthopedic Hospital and Medical Center in Seattle and as professor of pediatrics and health services at the University of Washington, with frequent trips to Washington, D.C., as an advisor to Senators Magnuson and Jackson of that state. He is one of the relatively few pediatricians with an abiding interest in child development and an understanding of both its complexities and the importance of its concepts to those who need to know children in order to provide for them most beneficially.*

I don't think there's any future for pediatricians in the next few years unless we shift our pediatric education. With the lowered birthrate, with the nurse-practitioners, and with the family physicians, what is left for the pediatrician to do? Well, I think that there are many things left for the general pediatrician to do in caring for children but right now the pediatrician isn't trained to do them. The key area is child development. That's something of assisting children and their families in learning problems . . . in development, in behavior. These are areas that the nurse-practitioner and the family physician are not going to be able to get into, and there is a tremendous void. But child development is not fashionable and the only way this can be turned around is that suddenly the powers that run medical education have to say, "This is important to train people in." We have to start teaching our pediatricians more about child development, or they won't be viable anymore.

GILBERT STEINER *Gilbert Steiner is a political scientist, senior fellow in the Governmental Studies Program of the Brookings Institution, where he assays various federal agencies, organizations, and programs in human services. He has followed the Comprehensive Child Development Act of 1971 in its meanderings through conferences, committees, coalitions, and finally, the halls of Congress and the White House. His* The Children's Cause *is a study of governmental responsiveness to children.*

He was interviewed because of his perceptiveness, his original and provocative thought, and his pragmatic (for the most part) approaches to the solution of social problems.

I belong to the school that says the primary need of the largest single group of children in this country is for economic security. I would argue, therefore, on behalf of activity to ensure economic security through improved and simplified assistance mechanisms for low-income children. I would, at the same time, undertake to narrow in on the deficiencies in health care for children as well as the deficiencies in routine supervision— that is, what we have called in the past the day-care problem.

In order to try to accomplish change in those areas, I would move first toward federal justification for activity and with that in hand, if I could get it, I would worry over what I want to do first and try to create a widespread agreement on priorities of concern in the children's field. One problem we face is an increasing competition among proponents of the children's cause—the daycare people have their thing and feel especially strong about it, and even within the day-care movement there are those that are dedicated exclusively to fighting off proprietary day care, while others are dedicated to the creation of a network of publicity supported systems, and there are those who are dedicated to closing up substandard day-care centers, and still others are dedicated to opening up more day-care centers without regard to the niceties of the standards. But all of these groups are, in many ways, in competition with the people who are preoccupied with child nutrition, who are in turn in competition with the people preoccupied with child-health issues.

I am persuaded that unless we can move toward an agreement on what comes earliest and what can wait a little while, the child advocates will find themselves cutting each other up and making no advances whatever—which takes me back to the explanation of why I am so sorely disappointed in the activities of the various commissions and committees that have inquired into developmental theory but not into program priorities on behalf of children.

JOAN COSTELLO

It seems to me that our conceptions of inequality and where they come from in this society are very much at the heart of the unsolved problems of children, particularly poor children, children in minority or subordinate castes. So often child-development researchers or others concerned with children think that if we only understood more about development we could do things for children directly. And I think a lot more of us are aware now that the structure of our society is such that inequality is built in. No matter what we do for an individual child, children are growing up in a society that has a rhetoric about equality and equity and a social system that does not permit its emergence as a reality.

SALLY PROVENCE

I am absolutely convinced that day care can be helpful to people if you do it well, and if they need it but also that most of it is done rather badly; and a lot of it, I think, is frankly dangerous. I really am very concerned about the national bandwagon for day care as a right, or as a need. Along with a lot of concerned people, I think if we aren't going to do it well we are just very foolish . . . to push it so. To do it well you have to have enough people to provide for the developmental needs of the children and people cost money. So it means it's expensive to do.

I think we need all kinds of better services. My bias, and I guess that's why I am so involved with young children and young parents, is that it does seem to make sense to me that if you can start early and you can provide supports early, you just have a better chance of having that family develop well than if you wait until they have been in trouble for five years, or the child is delinquent, or the parent is in a mental hospital, and then try to intervene. I understand and sympathize with the people who are concerned about delinquency or about adult mental-health problems, or crime, or whatever, because they are terribly important too, but I can't see that we are going to get very far if we don't begin with the early years and do a good job of that.

8 What Tactics Can Help to Change America's Policies toward Its Children?

Those in high places are more than the administrators of government bureaus. They are more than the writers of laws. They are the custodians of a nation's ideals, of the beliefs it cherishes, of its permanent hopes, of the faith which makes a nation out of a mere aggregate of individuals. They are unfaithful to that trust when by word and example they promote a spirit that is complacent, evasive and acquisitive.

*Walter Lippmann, as quoted by
James Reston in* The New York Times

ORVILLE G. BRIM, JR.

The improvement of the child's lot, in my judgment, should take two modes of expression. I'm talking about the improvement *now* in getting more money applied to children's needs, rather than about the generation of more information about child development and the alteration of public policy on a long-term basis. One is the whole development of child-advocacy law which uses existing law plus what data we can gather . . . then uses these data to force the application of existing law so that sentences, or rulings, or administrative rulings, follow which redeploy existing money from one source to another. When you have a ruling like this you can't really say it's not in the budget because if the judge says you have to do it then you have to find the money and that means that something else gets short-changed. In this case it's a zero-sum game in which the money for children comes out of the money for something else and it's that kind of political contest enforced by a legal ruling. I'm very much in favor of this. I'm a strong supporter of it. It dislocates the system and people complain about the dislocation; indeed, it's designed to dislocate the system. That's what the point is because the advocates don't think the system works.

Secondly, there is the more common, more familiar, political process—public consciousness-raising and the transformation of this consciousness-raising into political action. For example, the child-abuse issue, which has surfaced in public consciousness very rapidly in the past four years, brought about legislation and the tax funds now being reallocated to child abuse are hopefully not from other child concerns but from other aspects of the budget. So those are the two direct actions. I do not know as much about the redesign of existing institutions, like health-delivery services, and the like, as I do about these two things.

I think what we need to do in our thinking is to continue to stress a proper balance between the realistic and the practical political and legal steps taken now on behalf of today's children, but not at the expense of throwing all our resources into action now, and concern for the children of the future. There is need for basic research and reformation of the society more generally in terms of children's institutions. Anything we can do to dampen the wild swings from one extreme to the other in the child-development effort would be worthwhile.

JUSTINE WISE POLIER

Remedies will depend on the ability to turn things around politically so that the welfare of children will in fact be given far higher priority at every level of government. To achieve this I believe it is necessary to continue to do hard fact-finding concerning unmet needs of children, to present the facts to larger segments of the community, and to coordinate all possible sources of strength for social change. Lack of awareness on community levels of what is not being done for or what is being done to children is one of the most awesome barriers which must be broken down. This means the development of child-advocacy groups that should include the consumers of services, citizens and professionals. At the same time selected cases must be pressed in the federal courts when violations of the constitutional rights of children are presented. Such cases will involve issues of equal protection, right to privacy, cruel and unusual punishment, the right to appropriate care and treatment, right to education, including the right to special education, the right to independent counsel, etc.*

MARIAN WRIGHT EDELMAN

What we've got to do now is simply give folks a program to rally around and do that hard community organization out there that's going to inform folks about specific bills and get them corralled and get them beginning to line up their Con-

* This statement, supplementing her interview, was made in a letter to Milton Senn.

gressmen so that they will not be able to vote against them. And I think you can do it. I just think it's hard. And one of the sad things is it's so hard to get just pennies to do this kind of organizational work around a key legislative issue. And we've just got to affect givers in a way that says $20,000 to organize around child development is more important than giving it to a campaign that's going to lose for some political candidate that makes you feel a little more powerful by association.

It can be argued that parents have not been very good advocates for themselves . . . or for their children. It seems to me we've got to provoke a national debate. I think you do that around very concrete, specific issues that you choose, that you try to get issues that as many people as possible can identify with and you use those as vehicles by which people can understand their own problems affecting kids and families here.

I think a broad children's lobby per se around kids is not going to work. I think you're going to have to take very specific issues—maybe in the health area. The medical experimentation on children issue is a good one. I mean, it's what the press likes. I'm not sure it's *the* most important issue affecting children but how do you get folk thinking about child health if they're bored by the fact that all these millions of kids are not getting adequate care? Nobody cares. Early screening diagnosis is having a hard row to hoe. But how do you get people thinking about health in children? I think you have to pick a good public issue and expose it and then figure out your remedies, and follow up and stick with it until you hit pay dirt.

I just think we've got to try to get Senator Mondale to hold hearings and go into the regions. If he's going to stay in Washington nobody's going to know about it but the *Washington Post*. So what we've been trying to get him to do is hold family hearings . . . and really just have regular families come and say just what the problems are that they're having with their kids and how they're trying to survive and how governmental policies are. You know you've had your Margaret Meads and you'll get your Jerry Kagans and that's fine. But it seems to me the more important role for that committee is just to have ordinary families talk about what a hard time they're having surviving in the country today. I think we've got to figure out how we can . . . be concrete, get good press, and give some payoff to the politicians. And I think that there are some issues on which that combination of factors can be put together. And again, if we can begin to educate the press. We've been trying to identify those ten key press folk whom we could even invite to sit in on our meetings, to get a real feel for what the problem is so that you can get an educated coverage when you do issue a report.

I think people *do* care about kids. I think they want at least to appear to care about them. Once we can begin to expose the fact that we are *not* child-oriented, that we are hypocrites and begin to make it understood that the traditional family (if there ever was such a traditional family) is not adequate to cope with today's problems . . . we may be able to begin to do something. But it means a long hard road. It took twenty years to get *Brown*. I think it's going to take a lot of years, too, just to provoke real, lasting reforms for children. But I think there has to be permanent, systematic advocacy that tries to bring together a number of people doing a number of different things. In the White House conferences, you know, you can't pronounce every ten years because there have been no specific follow-up mechanisms. And I think you have to pick out specific things and say, "We're going to do just that." And then stick with it till we do it.

CAROLYN HARMON *Carolyn Harmon was fitted for her unique role in the early days of the Office of Child Development by training in political science and child development. She was an important associate of Edward Zigler, director of the OCD, in planning legislation for federally supported day care. She is senior associate consultant for Lewin and Associates, Inc., Washington, D.C.*

One lesson certainly to be learned from the veto of the Child Development Act is that the academic establishment . . . and the child-development activists who head the major associations for children spent too much time in talking to each other and not enough time in finding ways to mobilize and inform public opinion. This was a rather low-saliency issue to most of the population, including most of the population that would benefit from it. No effort really seriously was made to bring out the climate of public opinion that would have made it really difficult or embarrassing for any president to veto this kind of legislation. Nothing happened. You can make an issue if you try hard and go about it in the right way. But the groups supporting this issue simply did not do that.

They could have used some of the time-honored strategies of really directing one's local chapters of whatever the organization might be to call this to the attention of its membership, make it a high-priority issue really for the organization, not one of a whole list of issues that are of interest. If this can be agreed upon, if you can start holding public forums, if you work on your local newspaper, on your editorial writers, if you try to see that this gets on the local television and in other media, if you engage in telephone campaigns and a whole gamut of activities that people can and do engage in on issues in which they choose to engage in that intensively, you can bring about a high degree of interest. And certainly this one had a lot of potential, because as the bill was written it would not be something that the affluent are doing for the poor. It was something that would have benefited probably 50 percent of the families of the country.

JOSEPH REID

I think it's obvious today that we are going to attain a lot of progress from the concern for the abused child, or the "battered" child, as it's known in medical circles. And it's quite evident that we are going to have some political campaigns developing with this as a focus; and here is an area that I think is extremely potentially productive for truly interdisciplinary work. For we know very little about the abusing parent and what causes abuse. If anyone had told me ten years ago that you could use the Alcoholics Anonymous pattern in working with the parents of an abused child I would have said they were crazy. But it's very obvious that we know very little about this pattern and I'm very hopeful that as we broaden some of the very excellent work that has been done by physicians in Denver and New York who have concentrated on a small segment of abused children—the very severely physically battered child to the hundred times larger problem of the child who is neglected and abused by parents that we can bring together the concern of the child-development people, the social workers, who have been in this area for a hundred years, the physicians, etc. to overcome this absolute dead spot we got on. We started out with organizations concerned with both abused animals and children. And, though the money rolled in for cats and dogs, it was almost nil for children. I'm hopeful that a concern for abuse, which so angers and frightens the body politic, may redirect their concern for all children. Just as in years past we've had concern over mental retardation or emotional disturbance, or some other form of need of children, I hope that this can be an entrée into a broader look at those protections we need for children in the United States and elsewhere.

For example, I think perhaps day care has been mined out today; it's going to be very difficult to mount real major legislative efforts again. But we may get back to day care through the examination of child abuse and its implications and its widespread danger because fortunately, whereas Head Start was tarred by being for the poor child, abuse as we know it cuts through all levels of the population. It is not just a symptom of the very poor or black, etc. and it may interest people then in those social provisions that have to be made to sustain all families in the United States and particularly to sustain the mother who leads such an isolated existence in our average family.

We still haven't found that rubric under which we can get the total public interested. But I've been very interested in talking about child abuse to, for example, two senators a few weeks ago. One was saying, you know, "these horrible people." And I simply asked if they had children, and they said, "Yes." And I said, "Well, did you ever, when you had an infant and you were walking the floor for the fourth night at two o'clock in the morning, feel like taking that kid and throwing him against the wall?" And both of them sort of looked at each other, and the first one said, "Well, yeah, I do remember that." And I said, "Well, that is a natural experience for everybody. Now just put yourself two or three degrees more disadvantaged, under more pressure, and you can imagine yourself abusing a young child, can't you?" I think here we've got the possibility of talking to *everybody* because practically every parent, if he really thinks about it, remembers a time when he could have abused the child or did abuse the child.

There is one group of legislators that you will only get interested in an issue if you can get them through the route of cost-effectiveness. It's going to cost them more if they don't do it. But there's another group which, if you can get them involved on a minimal basis, if you can get them to go look at a day-care center, for example, or if you can get them to look at three abused children being brought to a hospital, their humanness gets them involved. We professionals are our own worst enemies in all of this. When it comes to legislation for children it is essentially a "no win" situation for the legislator. There are a few people who are going to vote for him because he voted for some child-welfare thing. But since we professionals are usually fighting over what's best and who gets it, etc., he usually gets some negative votes out of it. And I think our inability to not promote our own panaceas to the exclusion of everything else, particularly around some of these big issues like the child-development issues and day-care issues in recent years, has usually put the legislator in a position of having to make choices and make choices which he knows are only going to work to his detriment.

In a certain sense I think what we have been going through as a country in terms of youth and drugs, etc. has made a tremendously larger and important segment of the population aware of children's needs—particularly the upper middle class, which is so influential in terms of voting, for it's a rare person that hasn't had a child in his immediate family who has been caught up in the whole question of alienation, drugs, etc. So that I think that we are in a stage of our history where with the right exploitation we can go a lot further than ever before. Far more people are conscious of the terrible effects of general neglect on children.

WILLIAM SMITH

All you need in terms of legislative process—at least in my perspective—is enough, shall we say, sexy facts and statistics to give to the politician who makes the speech to persuade other politicians and other policymakers that (a) there is a problem and (b) there is something politically practical that can be done about it.

The unique thing about the crusade against hunger is that, at least in my limited experience here in Washington the last ten years or so, it's the only moral crusade that I know of that has worked. At least it was moderately successful. I've been trying to figure out for the last four or five years how to duplicate that experience and I haven't found another issue on which you can have the same success. We did use in that effort scientific studies about . . . what happens to a child's brain when he doesn't have enough protein before he is five years old. All we needed for that was to demonstrate that a child below a certain age needs protein and if he doesn't get protein his brain is damaged. You didn't even have to ask why; you didn't even have to go behind the conclusions; to assert it was enough.

The scientists were effective. Look at who they were. I think almost all of them, if not all of them, were practicing pediatricians who went out and looked at children and examined children clinically out in the field where they lived, in their homes, and that effort by the scientists, who then came and testified to what he or she had found, was then duplicated by the politicians and members of the committees who went out and saw the deprivations for themselves and put it on nationwide television, get everybody exercised about it. And at that point you've got a viable issue.

Maybe you have to be satisfied with the solution to the individual problem. The crusade against hunger was really only a piece of the whole poverty problem.

ABRAHAM BERGMAN

In the Congress there are so many important issues . . . and so when one works on behalf of children one has to make the case with the people who make the decisions. And this is where advocates of children have done far too much speaking and writing about the righteousness of the case without getting their hands dirty in actual accomplishment. Just preaching about righteousness really isn't going to get us anywhere. Whether we like it or not, we have to reach the people who have the power and interest *them.*

Now the combination that I try to work in politics is to pick an idea that is right, the right thing to do, *and* is politically advantageous to the particular politician. I don't go to a politician and ask him to do something that's going to lose him votes or get him defeated. And I also try and point out that there are advantages of working on behalf of children because even though children don't vote their parents do and that it is possible to forge a political campaign on the basis of what one does for children.

Don't try and decide beforehand whether a politician is a good guy or a bad guy. Many people try and write off certain individuals because they're from one party or another party and say, "I don't want to go talk to him." The nice thing is that health really is a nonpartisan issue. I've never seen it come down on the side of Republicans versus Democrats. If you take an issue to somebody, if they think it is a good issue, if they see it is going to be feasible, they're going to go for it—if they don't gain too many enemies. You see, that was the problem with the day-care legislation. The day-care legislation was beautiful stuff but I'm amazed that it went as far as it did. And it went as far as it did because a very effective coalition kept it a low-profile issue. You have to decide in the beginning whether you need publicity to help. In many of my causes I need the publicity; the politician needs to have credit for the things he does and so you need to gain attention for the fact that Senator Jackson is working on Indian health legislation, for instance, or that Senator Mondale is working on sudden-infant-death legislation. This is something very necessary to the process. But the day-care legislation had to be kept low profile, and of course a large issue like that can't remain low profile. As soon as the implications of it surfaced, then the kooks came out of the woodwork and it became an unsafe issue. It became something where a congressman previously said, "This sounds like a good idea," then after the publicity said, "My God, this may get me into trouble." The legislation was made into an issue of disruption of the American family and thought control, and the barrage of publicity came down on it. And I think it was inevitable that the thing was vetoed. It was an idea ahead of its time.

An area I'm working in now is health education. I was just in Washington yesterday talking to Congressman Meeds of the state of Washington. He has introduced this legislation in the area. Here's how the process works. The PTSA's approached Congressman Meeds—he is ranking Democrat on the Education Committee—and said, "We need something in school health education," and they helped him draft a bill that he introduced last year. Congressmen, you know, introduce thousands of bills and they don't get anywhere. Meeds didn't put that much effort into the legislation because he had some other priorities ahead of it. I happened to see the bill just by accident and said, "My God, this is magnificent," I saw the congressman last year and said, "Do you know how important this thing is that you introduced?" He said, "No." Its importance is this: we talk about health, but medical care doesn't have that much to do with health. If we want to do something about dental disease, heart disease, cancer, drug abuse, these sorts of things, we have to do it outside of the doctor's office. The problems are influenced by habits of living, nutrition, exercise, things like that. And one place we can influence lifestyles is in the schools. Health education, in many places, consists of one lecture a year on sex by the gym coach before the kids graduate from high school. So this bill is to provide for training of teachers to do it and then federal assistance to school districts who will provide innovative school health programs.

Now what I was doing yesterday was telling Congressman Meeds and his staff how to make this issue gain some visibility, make it "sexy." The issue was really that of preventative medicine, another slogan that people mouth but nobody does anything about. And I told them, "Look, if you say this is real preventative-medicine education, then it is going to get the attention of colleagues and it might start to fly." I put them in touch with the American Academy of Pediatrics and said that if this relatively conservative body comes and backs something, that is going to reassure congressmen. You see, anything you want to get through has to find the middle ground. This gets back to what I said before—preaching and the morality or the righteousness of issue doesn't help. You have to reach congressmen who are basically middle-of-the-road, and you have to make it appeal to them. And if you can't do that, then forget it. It isn't going to happen.

LEONA BAUMGARTNER

Politicians are just like other people. You have definitely to sit down and level with them what you want to do. Explain the facts. You have to do two or three things. I think number one you have to know your subject very well and you have to have facts and you have to know which ones to choose. You can have pages of statistics and if you give it to them they won't listen at all. But you have two or three and then maybe if a guy asks a question, you can deal in a couple of more. You have to play this like mixing a salad or something or other. You have to have humor. They're used to having people (at least in my experience) that come and pound the table and say all kinds of things. I took it for granted that every one of them was just terribly interested in all the people in New York and wanted to do good. They wanted to do good by all the babies in New York and the Health Department was one thing that was always everybody's friend in New York and now we just needed a little bit more help to do a better job. If they put up this much money this is what we expected we could do for them—not for us, for *them* and for the City of New York.

Wagner got elected, and Wagner went after me for commissioner [of health] and I turned him down a couple of times and then finally went. That was 1954. I was in very well with the mayor and I had a definite technique with him. I saw him not often. When I saw him, I had a typed agenda; I knew the things that I wanted to get done the most. I had some things on there that could wait over because the mayor is under tremendous pressure. I judged him a little bit as to how tense he was when I walked in. I always had a couple of good stories for him—stories about accomplishment of the Health Department. While he sort of drew his breath . . . because he'd been out all over town, I'd say, "Bob, do you want a couple of stories for some of your speeches?" So I was offering him something. And then I came back with what I wanted him to do. When he saw he needed help he would send me over to the Board of Estimate.

I didn't go to the Board of Estimate with drama moods in general because I think that doesn't pay dividends over a long time. They hear too much drama. They see too much drama. I think if you know what you want to get done and if you know why it's important to get it done and if you know what good it's going to do, if you can make it happen and know what the price tag is, and if you're willing to compromise a little bit, you can almost always get anything you want. At least this is my experience.

DONALD COHEN

Donald Cohen is a graduate of the Yale University School of Medicine, then trained in general and child psychiatry. He was special assistant to the director of the Office of Child Development soon after its inception. There he worked to improve the quality of federal programs for children and was an advocate of the rights of children too often neglected. He has continued to show his concern about the autistic child, by designing and carrying out original studies at the Yale Child Study Center focusing on the etiology and special characteristics of that and similar syndromes.

Groups come saying, "We want to be heard, we want input into policy, we have a lot to contribute." After you see society after society coming with the same comment you say, "Well, what would you like us to do?" And usually they are very unclear about what they would like you to do and, secondly, they are unwilling to say what kinds of solutions and changes they would make in the ways that things are currently functioning. And because they came with nothing very clear and didn't know how they would like to change current administrative policy—and because there was nobody within HEW to articulate it with them they—never got anywhere. I think that is the typical situation with professional groups which make the pilgrimages to talk to an agency chief. To be effective requires a very clear sense of what you want to do today, or what rules you want to change today. What new funding do you want, is it "doable," where do you take that money from? Lobbyists need to be explicit: "We should take the money from Maternal and Infant Health and put it instead into pediatric clinics for teenagers." The third element that is required for effectiveness is that somebody in HEW needs to be willing to carry the ball. Otherwise, the script will be like that of meeting after meeting I sat through: famous people come, one government official sits there, you nod, they have nothing to say, you have nothing to say to them, and they leave.

It seems to me that we really are in a very tough situation about what's going to happen to the Office of Child Development. OCD's major failing has been in its inability to integrate and coordinate all other services for children. In spite of all the rhetoric, what has been done at OCD during these last couple of years has been some very good programs of its own, improving the quality of the programs that we had, and some small advocacy efforts because of individual people's interests. What we've been very ineffective in doing has been to bring together any other people's programs.

My own sense is that whenever children's programs aren't clearly delineated and where there is not a real locus where people can lobby and know where they can be heard, children are going to get short shrift. It's to the advantage of children to have a program at the highest level of HEW that you can achieve which brings together, under one administrative aegis, children's services. I think it's really important. One often still hears from children's lobbyists, in spite of the fact that they should know better, that what they really want is an advocacy group that has no services. And what they have in mind can easily become a nice old pediatrician or social-welfare person working in the Social and Rehabilitation Service with four or five staff people; as an advocate in the old Children's Bureau mold, she'd have a very powerful voice, and she'd run the risk of having nothing accomplished. My sense is that unless OCD controls programs, really has some say on how programs are going to be run and on allocation of resources, that we won't be able to do anything for children.

If I were asked what would I want, I would lobby for at least three new things: that OCD should administer Title IV-A day care, the largest federal day-care program; again administer Maternal and Infant Health and Medical programs; and administer a newly funded comprehensive child care program.

EDWARD ZIGLER

I don't think good things are going to be accomplished by agencies or even advocacy groups for children. I have been a member of such groups—I'm in the center of them—and unfortunately what I have discovered in my two years in Washington is that we are too fond of talking to each other. I would think that what must happen in this nation is more of an educational campaign, that what must be recruited is not one more advocate in our field but some journalists and television programs. We need a real rising national awareness. Otherwise, I think all that we're going to see is some more commissions. Every ten years we'll have a White House Conference documenting the same inadequacies that we documented ten years before, and there'll be very little progress forward.

I think that there should be advocacy groups. I'm not saying that they do nothing. I think that we do all we can to keep congressmen honest on these child and family issues that we're interested in, that we use whatever wallop we have, and that professional organizations take it upon themselves to become a little more political than they have been willing to become in the past and make themselves heard. But at the same time I think the critical matter is going to be educating that voting citizen in Iowa, and throughout the nation. Once the people decided going to the moon was a good idea, we went to the moon, and if we can ever convince people in this country that spending money in behalf of children, mounting programs in behalf of children, is the thing to do, Congressmen will get the message and we will do it.

The really first-rate people who write for popular consumption are very, very few. Robert Coles, of course, is an exception. You find his books everywhere. But what I'm saying is that instead of writing two or three more articles for professional journals, some of our leading, respected, figures, who will not perpetrate some of the nonsense that some of our "experts" put into magazines, have got to take the lead and write for popular consumption.

Certainly I think that this nation hasn't begun to develop the kinds of places where people are concerned with social policy for children. We have no Brookings Institution for children. You know, we don't have groups sitting around the country trying to combine knowledge about children and what the social-policy implications of that knowledge might be. In the old days of the institutes, you know, nobody was concerned about social policy for children then. That wasn't the concern of the child institutes of the thirties and forties, but I think now is the time when a child institute can take on this job. These should be places where this is pursued—in some of our rich centers around the country: Yale, the group at Harvard, the group at Minnesota, the group at Stanford. They ought to be actively adding onto their child faculties these kinds of economists and social-policy people that could finally use these scarce resources explicitly to help in the development of social policy.

We had the White House Conference on Children in 1970 and one of the requests was a cabinet rank for children. Well, that's good rhetoric and makes people feel very righteous, but establishing a cabinet position in Washington—a new department—is just about an impossibility. I just do not see a department for children. I see, hopefully, a future successful Office of Child Development. I think what might also be ideal is if we had a president who was so committed to children that he had a counselor . . . whose "thing"—expertise—was children, that would be of great value. So that what I would see as probably the most that people interested in children and families could hope for realistically is a situation where we had a strong Office of Child Development in the Secretary's Office, with a nation committed to its success and a counselor sitting in the White House whose special concern was children and who had the ear of the president.

NICHOLAS HOBBS

I am fairly well convinced that we have a very poor pattern for developing federal policy and state policy in respect to children or to family life and child development. We have used commissions and committees. The commissions tend to be highly political in character with a good bit of trade-off so that you don't offend the psychologists or the social workers or the psychiatrists or someone else. There's a dampening down, modulation of recommendations, so that people aren't offended.

I think the main thing we need is the old child development research stations revised, as it were, with a modern cast to them, with some interest in political problems. Our project on classification of exceptional children will recommend that there be established in the nation at least a half-dozen centers that will focus on public policy as it pertains to family life and child development so you can get some continuity, build some staff with the talent that's required. The commissions and committees that meet and say something and dissolve, I think, are very ineffectual ways to shape national policy.

GILBERT STEINER

Child-rearing is the least regulated important aspect of American life. One of the reasons for this is that there has been no systematic effort to create or defend a theory that would suggest to public policymakers the conditions under which public intervention in parent and child affairs is appropriate, and the conditions under which public intervention may not be appropriate, so that we come to arguing each proposal on an ad hoc basis without a theory to guide us. Now, I think it is probably taken as an easily accepted proposition in most quarters that intervention is justifiable or that it is at least defensible in those circumstances in which a child is deprived entirely or parental support by virtue of the death of his parents or a prolonged physical or mental incapacity. That, in a sense, is the easy case because we know that there are relatively limited numbers of these most-unlucky children. We have also accepted as a given the idea of public intervention to prevent outrageous or frightful occurrence of physical problems—routine injections at birth and protection against incipient blindness; activities of this sort are readily enough accepted. To move, however, to the question of the problems that continue to face American children, I suggest that the first problem is the determination of what kinds of help are acceptable for governmental agencies at any level to provide to parents and to children and at what point, on the other hand, the privacy of the parent-child relationship continues to deserve protection. None of us, I think, are yet willing to say that public intervention is properly unlimited.

We have given very little attention to thinking through in our own minds and setting down on paper a set of guidelines that would help members of Congress and administrative officials, and persons in state and local agencies, as they confront this day-to-day question of what is within the appropriate boundaries of government activity and what is not. In my judgment we cannot affect change unless and until we know the direction of the change we are trying to achieve. And so I am wrapped up in a single idea here. I think there is a receptivity on the part of policymakers to change in the distribution of responsibility for children between government and private agencies but to operationalize that receptivity requires guidance; to address the questions of what kind of change to effect, who wants the change, and what the consequences of the change may be is a responsibility that falls on the shoulders of those who are moving toward change. I am not satisfied that we discharge our responsibility very satisfactorily.

Let me take a case in point; think, for example, of the great child-care efforts of the last ten years. You and I can remember that in the late sixties there seemed to be very good grounds to believe that government would have a significantly increased role in child-care arrangements in the United States. The federal agency dealing with children presumably was about to be upgraded, and the Congress was showing a profound interest in problems of child welfare and child care. A whole host of agencies around the country had been created with public and private resources to concern themselves with improving the condition of child care. I have been struck, however, by the fact that very little of it came to pass and one notion that I have had is that very little of it came to pass because, in the last analysis, there was not a high measure of agreement about the purposes of new activity in child care.

We thought increased public intervention in this field would rest on the desirability of enhancing early cognitive development and a good body of scholarly literature had been generated that suggested to some readers that intervention and early schooling would have a marked effect on cognitive development. That became one cornerstone of the child-care movement. But it was only one; around that same time other persons were persuaded that child care and public intervention in programs for child care were really the most satisfactory, the most rewarding way, to accomplish social change, community change, which is quite a different dish of tea from early cognitive development. And these were the activities associated with a good many of the community-action programs, the whole stream that commenced with the Mississippi Child Development Group and subsequent work along those lines focused on community change as the purpose of new activity in child care. It was also true that a whole different group of persons—persons of good will—worrying over the effect of prolonged dependency on children, viewed child care as what we have a tendency to refer to as a "merely custodial" enterprise that would facilitate an attack on prolonged economic dependency by making it possible for children's otherwise dependent parents to be employed. This was child care for the sake of welfare reform, or reduction in the cost of public dependency. These three streams of interest in child care—for cognitive development, for community change, and for economic independence—happened to come along at the same time, I think by coincidence as much as anything else, and joined for a little while in the public-policy arena. Together, they gave rise to a misleading notion that we were on the verge of a new era of public activity in child care.

Now, I think that that did not come to pass because in fact they were separate streams and they turned out really to be incompatible in many ways. Clearly, child care for welfare-reduction purposes was not really compatible with child care for community change, nor was child care for community change necessarily identical with the goals of the people who were interested in early cognitive development. The early cognitive movement itself subsequently came under challenge with some uncertainty about whether its first findings could be validated over the long haul.

The point I want to get to is that change in the political sphere, in terms of puglic policy at least, is most likely to be effected when we start with a theory around which groups and interests can coalesce rather than when we start with an objective that particular groups wish to pursue prior to the development of the theory. Starting with the objective—which was the case in the child-care movement—I think minimizes the likelihood that other groups and interests will flock to the cause. Starting with the theory maximizes the likelihood that other groups and interests will be attracted to the theory involved. There are two bases for activity in this kind of a field. One basis is social altruism, where there are large numbers of very decent, very good people, who are concerned about what happens to their fellow creatures and in particular they are concerned about what happens to children. The other basis is self-interest. One does not preclude the other. It is possible to adhere to a self-interest notion and also be possessed of social altruism but, by and large, they move in two different streams. Marian

Wright Edelman has made very effective use of the social altruism idea in organizing Junior League women to go down and expose the fact that there are children detained in adult jails in America. She is persuaded, I think properly, that it is the indignation of the Junior League women that is most likely to overcome this, not the indignation of the social activists like Marian Wright Edelman herself. At the same time, the self-interest cause is of tremendous significance. It is now possible to pinpoint a self-interest group in the field of child care. We are beginning to see the emergence of a fascinating self-interest activity in that field as the American Federation of Teachers discovers that it must reach out for new clients, so to speak. Albert Shanker has been working hard at trying to persuade his AFL-CIO colleagues that the AFT should be endorsed as a lead agency in pursuing preschool educational objectives. In effect, it would make it possible for Shanker to find jobs for the large numbers of primary-school teachers who are or will soon find themselves superfluous in a declining birthrate situation. That's an example, I think, of the possible uses of self-interest in accomplishing change on behalf of children. I don't shy away from it. I think it is the single most effective kind of mechanism to accomplish change and if it is possible to merge the groups and organizations pursuing self-interest with those that move along particular directions out of a sense of social altruism I think we will have a potent and useful kind of lobby activity. I think that merger can be effected if we first can pay enough attention to the problem of finding a theory of intervention and lay that theory out and then invite adherence to it from both the social altruists and the self-interest groups.

We have had several opportunities in recent years to develop theories of intervention and I find the most depressing single aspect of the child-development movement in this country to be that each of those opportunities has been a failure. We can explain the why of each of the failures but it is important to be aware of them. I remind you, for example, of the Joint Commission on Mental Health of Children with an initial $500,000 federal grant, and with a mandate that read, for all practical purposes, "Bring us a theory." Unhappily, the Joint Commission on Mental Health of Children brought us eight hundred pages of nontheory, not much else—and it was more than could be digested and in many ways was less than worth thinking about. Its apparent successor, the Human Services Institute, finds itself carrying on in precisely the same kind of disjointed fashion. We have had an opportunity through the years in a succession of White House Conferences on Children to attend to the question of theory. And I think you will have to go all the way back to 1909, the first one, to find a legitimate and reasonable and thoughtful concern with the development of theory. Since that time, there has been a steady escalation of the numbers of participants . . . and a steady diminution in the care and attention paid to fashioning a theory and a program with which large numbers of people can be comfortable. We have had an opportunity to develop a theory again in the activity that is still underway under the auspices of the National Academy of Sciences-National Research Council, and its Advisory Committee on Child Development. For divers reasons it has not itself been able to attend to this question although I believe that the first director the Office of Child Development ever had, your colleague Ed Zigler, had precisely this in mind when he invited the National Academy to create such a committee. Dr. Zigler was looking for a credo, a statement of what the director of OCD believed the appropriate role of government to be, and why that was an appropriate role, and hoped that the NAS/NRC people could help along those lines. He has long since gone from government, but the Advisory Committee is still struggling and trying to accommodate the different interests of its members.

I do not denigrate the work of the child-development departments around the various universities, but I think they tend to do better as students of one or another aspect of children's problems than they do as students of the problem of the philosophy of intervention. I think that it is more appropriate to fault the students of political and social science than it is to fault the students of child development in this connection. The child-development people in many ways are doing the job they set out to do—to advance knowledge about child development, to provide explanations as to what is likely to happen with any particular kind of intervention mechanism. Unhappily, the students of political and social science have not attended to the question of what are those social and political consequences, costs and benefits, of accepting the findings of the child-development specialists.

ROBERT ALDRICH

Young residents come in occasionally and ask my opinion and I tell them to go into politics if they really want to get anything done. I think that for the next ten or fifteen years we should be systematically preparing politicians who have a medical degree and a very good grasp of human growth and development, social and physical, who can take their place in the advisory and action bodies as state legislators, federal agencies, federal Congress and so on, and to have a voice there rather than always being in groups who are having to talk from the outside and who aren't a part of the action structure. If you really want to get anything done in child health to reverse the downhill trend, which I happen to believe is going on, I think it's going to require some people going into politics as a career.

WALTER MONDALE

The human-program professionals and researchers get at best D-minus for their recognition and involvement in the politics of children. Some have tried. But I have tried many, many times to get them generated and organized. I must say, the teachers are doing better than anybody now. They have become quite a force and it is a force that helps the teachers, but I think it also helps education and children. But welfare organizations I have not seen come up and show any political clout. And then you get into these incredible turf problems, as I call them. I remember a conference we had when we tried what I thought was getting a coalition to pass child-abuse legislation. To my dismay, they came together to fight over who was going to get the money and, in my impression, most of them would rather not have the program if the money wasn't going down their chute. And it's not a very pretty spectacle.

We have to keep trying to tap the tremendous political clout of the professionals in the field and get them to see—they are all good people—that it is not enough to help children personally, as important as that is. If every teacher and welfare worker and poverty worker and health professional and others involved —manpower specialists, penal, correctional officials, etc.— if they could all kind of gather together in a coalition for children and really make it work politically, that could be a big difference.

I think efforts for children ought to begin with the most manageable and most reasonable first step and that is that the professionals get together and start doing their job. They ought to solve those turf problems for us. They shouldn't come up here and hold us hostage for everyone of those professions. They ought to get together, lock themselves in a room, resolve their differences and say, "Here is our plan; we have designed it for the kids, not for ourselves." It's unfortunate that a lot of times, instead of that, they like us to do the compromising and then everybody stands back and criticizes. That's why a lot of people get out of this work. It's hard to have those knives in your back.

Secondly, I think we have to be more careful in our strategy in developing proposals. Too often our proposals smell of welfare and that average worker out there who is not on welfare and who can barely make it, who is paying taxes, and his wife often is working too, says, "Well, now, when is this going to stop? I am taking care of *my* kids." I have had friends of mine who represent auto-workers districts, Walter Reuther districts, who have had to abandon this fight, or at least diminish it, because they say, "Well, the public gets sick of this; they say, what's in it for us?" And there has been a form of elitism, I am afraid, in many of the proposals which has disgusted that great middle working group in American life whose support you must have if you are going anywhere. That's where George Wallace is making his inroads—partly because they think that their political leadership is not sensitive to that concern. For example, we recently pushed a bill for a $200 credit per dependent. We did not get exactly what we wanted but we got a $30 credit for all families which cost 5.8 billion and will mean $100, or $150, for the average family—nothing big but it is money that flows according to family size. It is the first time we have adopted something like a children's allowance. I hope it will stay in the law and we can begin to build on it. Now, that's a proposal where you can go to the auto worker and say, "Here is money for you and your family to help you in the problems that you have raising your kids and making the costs of it." It's got the right smell; it isn't welfare, it's tax relief. The more of that that we can shape the better so that we don't get into these divisions —poor or middle-class divisions—which have, in retrospect, been one of the worst dividends from the Great Society programs.

I have also pursued certain reforms which are not very costly . . . which I think we have got a chance of passing even over a veto. Child abuse, for example. That's a small part of a much bigger picture but we have now got child-abuse programs going and it was my opinion that we could pass that thing. I am sure Nixon wanted to veto it, but he didn't feel he could be for child abuse—nation abuse, but not child abuse! We did the same on sudden-infant-death research. We are going to hold some hearings now on adoption, baby-selling, trying to match the tremendous thirst for children and adoption with the number of children who need it, to see if there is some way of doing better in that area. What I am saying is, we are taking pieces of the problem that don't carry fantastic price tags which Americans can understand and which we might be able to pass even though we are in an environment where there is not a lot of sympathy for the overall objective.

Afterword

As this is written, the political campaign of 1976 has ended. It seems a particularly appropriate time for reflection, if not prediction, about what the future holds for America's children.

A first impression is pessimistic, the probability that the immediate future will bring no significant changes. The long and tedious political struggle, with its millions of words spoken and written, paid children scant attention. Their health, development, education, and well being—in fact, their being at all as individuals—did not become specific items for discussion or debate. The word *children* was seldom expressed, and when it was, it often held a negative connotation. One aspirant for the Senate recommended the abolition of child labor laws; pro-life exponents were anti-abortion rather than advocates of all living infants and children. Considerable attention was devoted to the juvenile offender, but the emphasis devolved on how to punish him and his parents rather than how to ameliorate their precriminal lives and problems.

A case may be made that politicians subsumed their interests in children and family under the rubric of "our people" when they put forth their ideas on the economy, inflation, health insurance, welfare reform, and unemployment. And it cannot be denied that these issues are basic to any consideration of the needs of all children. However, the campaign rhetoric proved what so many of the persons interviewed in this oral history believed, that since children do not constitute a political constituency they are without representation. Or, as one wit put it, "They are not tall enough to reach the lever in the voting booth."

What does this mean for the future? Will the future continue to be one of slow, hesitating change, acceptance of the status quo, benefits only to children of the affluent, neglect of the poor, drift because there is no leadership or direction from people in high office?

Progress may well continue to be measured by small changes for a while, it may be characterized by indecision. Yet there seems to me to be a groundswell of public opinion, general concern, anger, energy, and power ready to be activated by persons at the highest levels of our federal government.

At the time of my interview in 1975 with Senator Walter Mondale he had already earned bipartisan respect as a serious, diligent, and constructive legislator. He was the author of bills on child development and day care, child abuse and research into crib death. The last two are now federal laws. Extensive hearings which he conducted publicized the plight of migrant laborers and deficiencies in public education. With Senator Javits he was instrumental in establishing the Independent Legal Services Corporation to represent minorities and the poor. Even political opponents recognize him as fairminded and to be trusted with influence and potential power. These he will continue to have in increasing measure as vice president.

Social scientists believe America has found a new frontier: the rights of children, the natural sequence to the human rights struggles of the previous decades. There is agreement as to its low profile at the present time, as well as to its vigor as a movement, deriving considerably from legislation such as Mondale's child abuse bill and a variety of efforts by legal rights groups fighting especially for children. Among the latter is, of course, the Children's Defense Fund, directed by Marian Wright Edelman.

While the legal defenders presently are focusing much of their attention on children incarcerated in institutions illegally or without benefit of comprehensive examinations and treatment or consideration of alternative plans for their care, their scope is

AFTERWORD

broader. What they hope to establish is that *every* child has a right to a safe, stable home, a reasonable education, due process of law, and freedom from abuse and neglect.

Much future reform will no doubt come from identifying, exposing, and correcting the numerous injustices against children because these will come to the attention of the courts. All the children's rights activity in the last few years has involved the U.S. Supreme Court. That court has agreed to review at least five cases this term that deal with the constitutional rights of children. State legislatures are becoming involved in cases concerned with placement of children in jails for and with adults. State reformatories and prisons are being closed down and replaced with group homes, foster homes, and other residential centers for juveniles. Many of these changes are being made cautiously, tentatively, and wisely, experimentally. It is likely that the pace of change will accelerate if the innovations prove themselves both generally beneficial to children and economically feasible. The danger is that when good programs are costly they will be judged only in terms of amounts of money spent rather than as benefits to children, projects of excellent quality which in the long run may actually save money for communities.

Another hazard—a major one—is the tendency for the public to look for quick results, tangible change. Well-designed, competently, and honestly administered ventures for children have been terminated prematurely when expectations were exaggerated or unrealistic. Americans have a tendency to be impatient with projects aimed at social and economic change. We look for and demand instant success, the best money can buy. We will need to be more patient, slower to discard the new and venturesome, less tempted to change either projects or priorities lest we truly waste both money and human lives. Only through this patience—but a patience born of renewed determination—is there the possibility of moving our nation nearer to what America has long meant, here and afar: generosity to the weak and justice to the disadvantaged.

Chronology of the Child Development Movement, 1902–75

1902   A permanent U.S. Census Bureau is established.

1908   Congress passes legislation regulating child labor in Washington, D.C., but the majority of the states fail to ratify the constitutional amendment.

          The first Bureau of Child Hygiene is established by New York City. This move from private charity to public responsibility for the health care of children was a major step toward the assumption of a broad national responsibility by the federal government.

1909   President Theodore Roosevelt convenes the first White House Conference on Children, focusing on the care of those dependent and neglected. The smallest of such decennial conferences, it is credited with having made the greatest impact on the health and welfare of children. One of its major recommendations called for a federal children's bureau.

1912   The U.S. Children's Bureau is established by a law signed by President William Howard Taft. It is placed in the Department of Commerce and Law. In the next twenty-five years, probably the bureau's most successful period, it did substantial work in the fields of care of dependent children, child labor, juvenile delinquency, and child health.

1916   The National Research Council is formed as an operating arm of the National Academy of Sciences for making scientific resources available to the government.

1920   The beginning of decades of philanthropic foundation grants for child development. Often disbursed through the Social Science Research Council, funds were largely contributed by the Laura Spelman Rockefeller Memorial, Rockefeller Foundation, General Education Board, Carnegie Corporation, Russell Sage Foundation, and the Rosenwald Fund.

1923   Social scientists found the Social Science Research Council (SSRC), designed to stimulate greater interaction among the various disciplines, to improve the conditions of research, and to increase general understanding of the nature of the social sciences.

1930   American Academy of Pediatrics was founded. It became the most important influence on standards of child-health care, continuing education in pediatrics, educational material for parents, and sponsorship of special studies.

1935   Social Security Act is signed into law by President Franklin D. Roosevelt. Title IV provided for the general welfare by a system of old-age benefits and provision for the blind, dependent and crippled children, maternal and child welfare, public health, and the administration of unemployment compensation laws.

1939   Social Security Act amendments greatly extend and liberalize the program for the protection of families.

In the first use of federal funds for special-project grants, the Children's Bureau provides for state services to children with rheumatic fever and heart disease.

Food Stamp Plan to dispose of agricultural commodities begins in Rochester, N.Y.

1940   White House Conference on Children in a Democracy calls attention to inequalities in opportunities available to children and youth in rural areas, among the unemployed, and in low-income, migrant, and minority groups; declares "What we might wish to do for . . . [a] future President, we must be ready to do for every child."

CHRONOLOGY

1941   Lanham Act authorizes federal support for school construction in "impact areas."

Children's Bureau approves project medical care of wives and children of servicemen and sponsors conference on day care for children of working mothers.

1942   Congress authorizes emergency grants to states for day care of children of working mothers.

1943   Congress appropriates initial funds for Children's Bureau Emergency Maternal and Infant Care (EMIC) Program.

1946   National School Lunch Act provides for grants to states and territories to establish, maintain, operate, and expand school lunch programs.

National Mental Health Act provides for research on psychiatric disorders and methods of prevention, diagnosis, and treatment; authorizes establishment of National Institutes of Mental Health; programs conducted by NIMH are broadened by 1956 amendments.

1950   Mid-century White House Conference on Children and Youth takes as theme "How to provide each child with a fair chance to achieve a healthy personality"; paper presented to conference by Kenneth B. Clark on effect of prejudice and discrimination on personality development.

1952   Children's Bureau grants funds for special projects to develop and coordinate statewide programs for medical and social services for unwed mothers.

1954   In *Brown* v. *Board of Education* (347 U.S. 483) U.S. Supreme Court unanimously reverses the doctrine of "separate but equal" and rules that legal separation on the basis of race violates the Fourteenth Amendment; in separate ruling, lower courts are ordered to use "all deliberate speed" to admit Negro children to public schools.

Division of juvenile delinquency is established in the Children's Bureau.

1961   President Kennedy appoints Panel on Mental Retardation. Its report of findings and recommendations in 1962 was the basis for Kennedy's special message to Congress on mental illness and mental retardation.

1963   Congress amends the Social Security Act to assist states and communities in preventing and combating mental retardation.

Following President Kennedy's proposal in 1961 and congressional legislation in 1962, the Surgeon General establishes the National Institute of Child Health and Human Development as part of the National Institutes of Health to conduct research and training in maternal and child health, special health requirement of mothers, and in human development.

Following the report of President's Panel on Mental Retardation, President Kennedy proposes programs to prevent retardation and improve mental health; Congress passes Maternal and Child Health and Mental Retardation Planning Amendments to the Social Security Act establishing projects dealing with premature birth, infant mortality, retardation, neurological disease, and other problems of mothers and infants; Mental Retardation Facilities and Community Health Centers Construction Act provides for facilities for research and for expansion of services and training for mentally retarded.

1965   Head Start programs launched by Office of Economic Opportunity for the improvement of conditions of learning, social development, and health care of children of preschool age.

1966   Child Nutrition Act is passed, which retains school lunch and milk programs; act authorizes and provides financial aid for new breakfast program for schools in poor areas; food programs for children in economically depressed areas are expanded in 1969.

1967   Children's Bureau assigned to the Social and Rehabilitation Service of HEW.

Child Health Act adds three new types of medical-care project grants (infant care, family planning, and dental care) to Social Security Act; 366,000 expectant mothers receive maternity services and school children are screened to determine health conditions and needs.

1968 Congress further amends Elementary and Secondary Education Act to authorize federal support to regional centers for education of handicapped children and special centers for providing services to deaf and blind children; amendments also provide for recruiting personnel, distributing information on handicapped, giving technical assistance to education in rural areas, bilingual education, and dropout prevention.

Congress passes Juvenile Delinquency Prevention and Control Act to assist courts, correctional systems, schools, and community agencies in research and training to prevent, treat, and control juvenile delinquency.

Citizen's Board of Inquiry into Hunger and Malnutrition in the United States publishes *Hunger, U.S.A.*, documenting extent and complexity of malnutrition.

1969 Office of Child Development, under the auspices of HEW, is created by President Nixon. Secretary Finch of HEW orders the reorganization of child health and welfare programs and functions, and establishes a Board of Advisors on Child Development. Children's Bureau and Bureau of Head Start and Early Childhood are transferred to Office of Child Development.

1973 U.S. Supreme Court decides constitutionality of abortion.

1974 Child Abuse Act passed.

1976 A child care bill passed by Congress. Vastly modified version of the Comprehensive Child Development Act of 1971, vetoed by President Nixon.

Selected Bibliography

Beck, Rochelle. "White House Conference on Children: An Historical Perspective." *Harvard Educational Review* 43 (1973): 653–68.

Bloom Benjamin S. *Stability and Change in Human Characteristics.* New York: John Wiley, 1964.

Bowlby, John. *Attachment and Loss.* New York: Basic Books, 1969.

———. *The Nature of the Child's Tie to His Mother. International Journal of Psychoanalysis* 39 (1958): 350–73.

———. *Separation, Anxiety and Anger.* New York: Basic Books, 1973.

Brim, Orville, Jr. *Education for Child Rearing.* New York: Free Press, 1965.

———. "The Sense of Personal Control over One's Life." Address to Divisions 7 and 8, the Eighty-second Annual Convention of the American Psychological Association, New Orleans, September 1974.

Bremner, Robert H., et al. *Children and Youth in America: A Documentary History,* vols. 1–3. Cambridge, Mass.: Harvard University Press, 1971–74.

Bronfenbrenner, Urie. "Developmental Research, Public Policy and the Ecology of Childhood." A paper presented at the President's Symposium, "Interactions among Theory, Research and Application in Child Development," at the Annual Meeting of the Society for Research in Child Development, Philadelphia, March 31, 1973.

Caldwell, Bettye. "Child Development and Public Policy: Scientists and Citizens." *Comment* (American Academy of Pediatrics) 25 (1974): 10–12.

Clausen, John A.; Brim, Orville G., Jr.; Inkeles, Alex; Lippit, Ronald; Maccoby, Eleanor E.; and Smith, Brewster. *Socialization and Society*. Boston: Little, Brown, 1968.

Comer, James P., Poussaint, Alvin F. *Black Child Care*. New York: Simon and Schuster, 1975.

Edelman, Marian Wright, "An Interview with Marian Wright Edelman." *Harvard Educational Review* 44 (1974): 53–73.

Escalona, Sibylle, and Leitch, M. *Early Phases of Personality Development: A Non-Normative Study of Infant Behavior*. Evanston, Ill.: Child Development Publications, 1973.

Frank, Lawrence K. "The Fundamental Needs of the Child." *Mental Hygiene* 22 (1938): 353–79.

———. "Human Development—An Emerging Discipline." In *Modern Perspectives in Child Development*, edited by Albert Solnit and Sally Provence. New York: International Universities Press, 1963.

Goldstein, Joseph; Freud, Anna; and Solnit, Albert J. *Beyond the Best Interests of the Child*. New York: Free Press, 1973.

Hunt, J. McVicker. "The Psychological Basis for Using Pre-School Education as an Antidote for Cultural Deprivation." *Merrill-Palmer Quarterly of Behavior and Development* 10 (1964): 209–48.

Jencks, Christopher. *Inequality: A Reassessment of the Effect of Family and Schooling in America*. New York: Basic Books, 1972.

Jones, Mary Cover; Bayley, Nancy; MacFarland, Joan W.; and Hanzik, Marjorie P. *The Course of Human Development*. Waltham, Mass.: Xerox College Publishing, 1971.

Kagan, Jerome, and Klein, Robert E. "Cross-Cultural Perspectives on Early Development." *American Psychologist* 28 (1973): 947–61.

Kessen, William. *The Child*. New York: John Wiley, 1965.

———. *Childhood in China*. New Haven: Yale University Press, 1975.

Keyserling, Mary Dublin. *Windows on Day Care*. New York: National Council of Jewish Women, 1972.

Kohlberg, Lawrence. "Development of Moral Character and Moral Ideology." In *Review of Child Development and Research*, edited by M. L. Hoffman and Lois W. Hoffman, vol. 1. New York: Russell Sage Foundation, 1964.

SELECTED BIBLIOGRAPHY

Levine, Murray, and Levine, Adeline. *A Social History of Helping Services: Clinic, Court, School and Community.* New York: Appleton-Century-Crofts, 1970.

Light, Richard J. "Abused and Neglected Children in America: A Study of Alternative Policies." *Harvard Educational Review* 43 (1973): 556–98.

McGraw, Myrtle B. *Neuromuscular Maturation of the Human Infant.* New York: Hafner Publishing Co., 1973.

Mondale, Walter F. "A Statement on Federal Policies." *Harvard Educational Review* 43 (1973): 483–86.

Murphy, Lois B. *The Widening World of Childhood: Paths toward Mastery.* New York: Basic Books, 1962.

———, and Moriarty, Alice E. *Vulnerability, Coping, and Growth: From Infancy to Adolescence.* New Haven: Yale University Press, 1976.

Mussen, Paul H., ed. *Carmichael's Manual of Child Psychology.* 3d ed. New York: John Wiley, 1970.

Polier, Justine Wise. "The Child and the Law: Contemporary Situations in Juvenile Justice." *American Journal of Public Health* 63 (1973): 386–89.

Provence, Sally, and Lipton, Rose. *Infants in Institutions.* New York: International Universities Press, 1963.

Richmond, Julius B. "Disadvantaged Children: What Have They Compelled Us to Learn?" *Yale Journal of Biology and Medicine* 43 (1970): 127–44.

Richmond, Julius B., and Caldwell, Bettye M. "Child Rearing Practices and Their Consequences." In *Modern Perspectives in Child Development,* edited by Albert Solnit and Sally Provence. New York: International Universities Press, 1963.

Salk, Lee. *What Every Child Would Like His Parents to Know.* New York: Warner, 1973.

Schorr, Alvin L. *Children and Decent People.* New York: Basic Books, 1974.

Senn, Milton J. E., and Solnit, Albert J. *Problems in Child Behavior and Development.* Philadelphia: Lea and Febiger, 1968.

Solnit, Albert J., and Provence, Sally, eds. *Modern Perspectives in Child Development.* New York: International Universities Press, 1963.

Spock, Benjamin M. *Baby and Child Care.* 3d ed. New York: Simon and Schuster, 1976.

Steiner, Gilbert Y. *The Children's Cause*. Washington, D.C.: The Brookings Institution, 1976.

Stewart, Guy W. "The People: Motivation, Education and Action." *Bulletin of the New York Academy of Medicine* 51 (1975): 174–85.

Terris, Milton. "Breaking the Barriers to Prevention: Legislative Approaches." *Bulletin of the New York Academy of Medicine* 51 (1975): 242–57.

Weiner, Irving B., and Elkind, David. *Child Development: A Core Approach*. New York: John Wiley, 1972.

White, Sheldon. *Federal Programs for Young Children: Review and Recommendations*. Vols. 1–4. Washington, D.C.: U.S. Department of Health, Education, and Welfare, 1973.

Worsfold, Victor L. "A Philosophical Justification of Children's Rights." *Harvard Educational Review* 44 (1974): 142–57.

Index of Names

For biographical sketch see first page cited.

Aldrich, Robert (pediatrician, educator): 114, 148, 195

Baldwin, Alfred (psychologist): 97
Baumgartner, Leona (pediatrician, public health administrator): 92, 184
Bergman, Abraham (pediatrician): 166, 181
Brim, Orville G., Jr. (sociologist): 59, 105, 173
Bronfenbrenner, Urie (psychologist): 11, 149

Cohen, Donald (psychiatrist): 185
Comer, James P. (psychiatrist): 129, 153
Costello, Joan (psychologist): 123, 168

Edelman, Marian Wright (lawyer): 5, 94, 101, 154, 174
Eisenberg, Leon (psychiatrist): 21, 138
Elkind, David (psychologist): 61, 103
Escalona, Sibylle (psychologist): 22, 133

Gershenson, Charles P. (psychologist): 45, 80, 104

Harmon, Carolyn (political scientist): 176
Hess, Stephen (political scientist): 21
Hobbs, Nicholas (psychologist): 126, 145, 189
Hunt, J. McVicker (psychologist): 49, 124
Hymes, James L., Jr. (psychologist, educator): 4, 88

Kagan, Jerome (psychologist): 60, 75, 133
Keniston, Kenneth (psychologist): 29, 115, 152
Kessen, William (psychologist): 18, 48, 82, 110, 136

Lash, Trude (political scientist): 165
Levin, Tom (psychologist, community organizer): 23, 86

INDEX OF NAMES

McCandless, Boyd (psychologist): 68
McGraw, Myrtle (psychologist): 46, 89
Mead, Margaret (anthropologist): 146
Miller, Judith (legislative assistant, educator): 112
Mondale, Walter (politician): 35, 116, 138, 196
Murphy, Lois Barclay (psychologist): 51

Nash, Lola (child care center director): 19

Phillips, Martha (congressional staff member): 156
Polier, Justine Wise (jurist): 144, 174
Provence, Sally (pediatrician): 38, 169

Quie, Albert (politician): 145

Radke-Yarrow, Marian (psychologist): 161
Reid, Joseph (executive director, Child Welfare League): 52, 89, 177
Richmond, Julius (pediatrician): 112, 164

Salk, Lee (psychologist): 16, 62
Sapir, Philip (executive, The Grant Foundation): 90
Sauer, Peter (community organizer): 158
Schmidt, William M. (pediatrician): 25
Schoellkopf, Judith (psychologist, nursery school educator): 57
Schorr, Lisbeth Bamberger (political scientist): 3
Senn, Milton J. E. (pediatrician): Introduction, 44
Shakow, David (psychologist): 93
Smith, William (lawyer): 28, 180
Solnit, Albert J. (psychoanalyst): 118
Sontag, Lester (pediatrician, psychiatrist): 134
Spock, Benjamin (pediatrician): 7, 53, 165
Steiner, Gilbert (political scientist): 167, 189
Stevenson, Harold (psychologist): 135
Stolz, Lois Meek (psychologist): 58, 156
Sugarman, Jule (executive, federal and municipal agencies): 109

White, Sheldon (psychologist): 8, 77, 110, 137, 147
Wickenden, Elizabeth (social scientist): 12, 76, 151

Zigler, Edward (psychologist): 27, 98, 161, 187
Zimiles, Herbert (psychologist): 95, 116